HOME AGAIN

HOME AGAIN

JOSE YGLESIAS

ARBOR HOUSE
New York

Copyright © 1987 by Jose Yglesias
All rights reserved, including the right of reproduction
in whole or in part in any form. Published in the
United States of America by Arbor House Publishing
Company and in Canada by Fitzhenry & Whiteside Ltd.

Manufactured in the United States of America

10 9 8 7 6 5 4 3 2 1

Library of Congress Cataloging in Publication Data

Yglesias, Jose.
Home again.

I. Title.
PS3575.G5H6   1987   813'.54   86-28791
ISBN: 0-87795-913-7

For Lisa and Leonard Baskin, oh yes.

HOME AGAIN

ONE

I walked into the empty old house in Tampa and the phone was ringing. Who could it be? No one knew I had left New York. Peace, peace in my old age; that's all I wanted.

It was my cousin Tom-tom. He said, "What are you doing here?"

"Why are you calling here?" I said, hectoring like a Tampa Latin (we never called ourselves Hispanics) as if I hadn't lived my whole adult life away from that tacky, inquisitive town and family, and long ago turned into a real American, which is worse.

He made a temporizing, grumbling noise into the phone.

"You know Celia and Cuco have been dead four months," I said.

"I was at the funeral," he said. "Where were you?"

"There's nobody here now," I said, still taking his tack.

"That's why," he said softly, changing course on me. "I don't like to think of Aunt Mama's house all quiet and lonely. I call 'cause that way at least the phone rings."

"You're crazy," I said and chuckled a bit, for the first time in months.

Tom-tom laughed along for a second, and then slowly, but gathering momentum, he composed an eulogy of Aunt Mama, my mother, dead twelve years at least. He ended it with the same statement he made at every last encounter in our lives, a kind of unanswerable explanation for their closeness: "Aunt Mama and I were born the same day, November twenty-nine, you know."

"Twenty years apart," I said, denying him his claim, bastard that I am.

"I was the oldest nephew," he said. "She was my youngest aunt."

He waited me out and I finally said, "You were her favorite nephew," giving her back to him, what the hell.

"You're so smart," he said. He had said that many times. Six times, to be exact. Each time I had come visiting after I published my first book thirty years ago. More drawn out again: "You're so smart."

"Yeah," I said.

"Today is November twenty-nine," he said. Then he yelled at his wife Olivia without protecting my listening ear. "I'm talking to Pinpin, for Christ's sake, don't scratch yourself, use the salve!" To me: "She never does what the doctor tells her."

"Listen, Tom-tom, I just walked in," I said.

"How does the place look?" he said, refusing to let go.

I was standing in the doorway of the kitchen, using the wall phone there, and I looked at the dining room and the living room ahead of me and at the open front door. It framed a super-realist picture of a patch of the four-foot-deep front yard planted with coarse Florida lawn grass; beyond it the bright sun made a tarred spot in the street glisten, and beyond that Corona's front porch across the way. A young black walked on the balls of his feet on Corona's sidewalk, his face turned towards our door as if he were peering into mine. More likely, he was staking out the house.

Mother, Celia, Cuco, everyone used to say you cannot leave the screen door unlatched, the front or back door unlocked. Christ, there wasn't going to be any peace here for me either.

I'd be ruled by those dead voices and the deteriorating neighborhood. You can't run away: the tritest, most worn-out wisdom of rotten movies and worse novels.

One final cliché: those dumb, wised-up heroes let you know—or their hack creators did—that they were, by God, going to start over again. Not me, I didn't want that. I was not returning, touching base, none of that. No swelling movie music for me. I was staying here for good and myself deteriorating as fast as I could. Tampa was where I came from; that's all you could say for it.

Note this: this is a fact. I'm a writer and I tend to talk fiction, but the following is fact: I am at the end of my tether, I am desperate.

Zing—standing there with the clean white phone in my hand (who kept it so clean these last months?) I got my terrifying airy feeling (it was mine alone) of total despair. My body lost its plumb, its density, its feeling of belonging to me. I had never heard of its happening to anyone, not even in literature, only to me. Coming down here, breaking all ties, holing up, that had done it—I was in outer space without an umbilical line. And no one strong enough to draw me back. I blinked and blinked and blinked: nothing took on substance. I came to on a kitchen chair, and I thought, I must not be entirely weightless: I had lowered myself into this chair.

You cannot wipe out all your knowledge and experience and then hope to start anew. You'd be an infant in an ungraspable world. You have to bring something with you, some little knowledge, a truth around which gather the barnacles of life. I didn't have it; I didn't want it.

Dixie Lee was Bing Crosby's first wife. That's all I could remember and it would have to do. I took a deep breath.

The phone rang. It was Tom-tom; I must have hung up on him. He said, "Is the phone working as bad in New York with this A T and T thing?"

"Tom-tom," I began.

"Wait, wait, I'll forget. How'd you get to the house?"

"I'll call you later," I said.

"I mean, did you drive down or did you fly and then take a taxi or did you rent a car?"

"A taxi."

"Then I'll come pick you up."

"No, no, I got to unpack and settle in."

"Settle in?" Tom-tom said. "You here for more than a couple of days? Goddamnit, damn it, I got eleven brothers and sisters and fifteen cousins and—"

"Tom-tom," I said.

"Don't question my figures. I got nothing to do but count them up. I got fifty nieces and nephews alone. A lot of good. They didn't bother to tell me you were here. And my fifteen cousins got thirty, thirty-two kids. I'm coming right over. You got to eat. Olivia can still cook. They never tell me anything. You think you can depend on family, you can't. But you can depend on me, Pinpin—remember when I was a counterman and I got you the dishwasher job? It was much better during the Depression. We saw each other, we were real cousins. I can still cook. A little. Roast beef, anyway. I'm coming over and pick you up."

"Tomorrow," I said and started to hang up but I could hear him talking fast and furious and brought the phone back to my ear.

"I have to talk to you about iron grilles for the windows. You got to have them or they'll break in and steal the furniture. Iron grilles like they put on the new Spanish restaurants. Not for fancy, for protection. And a wire mesh on the front door glass. All Cuco and Celia had was regular locks and a spotlight on the backyard. That's not enough. Not since Mariel."

He was out of breath.

I quickly repeated, "Tomorrow," and hung up. What a mess. Two steps into the living room and the phone rang again.

"Actually, I had an idea from Marina that you might be coming," he said the moment I picked it up. "Don't treat me like this. I call all my cousins and brothers and sisters all the time. Once a week. We get unlimited local calls in Tampa. But they're all too busy. Pinpin, I have to talk to you. You were always the smart one in the family. You made a living just sitting at your desk. Your own desk. In your own home. Remember, I asked you once?"

He laughed and wheezed and coughed.

"Look at me, with this apartment house. I got to look after it by myself. Olivia can't help. It takes all her energy not to scratch. Scratch! You better believe it. They got that sign says Children Playing and they don't let me take it off. I got to talk to you about that, too."

"Give me an hour," I said. "Give me an hour to unpack."

"Sure. Sure, you need time to think," he said, mollified, the anxiety in his voice disappearing like a radio turned off. "Do me a favor, think about the Children Playing. Think how I can put it nicely, humbly to the police—I always say a thing humbly the first time round. I'm not like some people come in punching. What was I saying?"

"We'll talk about it later."

"Oh, Children Playing. How to explain to them that it ruins my business if people think there are brats around making a lot of noise. The Police Department doesn't care. They leave it to the Traffic Department to decide. There are no children in my apartment house—Olivia wouldn't have them. I was going to take the sign off but the American wouldn't let me. It's my property, he says, my property—"

"What American?" I said and immediately regretted it.

"The one across the street. West Tampa isn't what it used to be, Pinpin—it's full of Americans."

He sighed so loudly that he would not have heard me say good-bye.

"It's not his property, it belongs to the city. The sidewalk to the curb belongs to the city. But do you think the city takes care of it? No, I got to plant the grass and then mow it the way they like. The time I was sick, those bastards from Pride came by and bothered Olivia. The weeds were too high and it didn't look good for the neighborhood. She told them a thing or two. It was better than scratching."

He laughed the low rumbling laugh that was his real laugh: it said, you made a mistake about me, buddy, I know a thing or two.

"Pride?" I said, curious like the writer I once was.

"Something they made up to clean the neighborhoods. It's a racket. They don't *pay* for anything, they just needle you, you know. And they have people of the other race to come tell you what you got to do."

Time was, and Tom-tom knew it, I would have said something angry about race prejudice.

When he got no rise from me, he hurried to explain. He needn't have—I let people be now, and everyone more or less returns the compliment.

He said, "They're just doing a job, I know that, and I'm glad colored people are getting all the jobs. But that son of a bitch doesn't own that sign and he takes no care of his yard. In fact, lousy. I was in the hospital, but I told Olivia, you look see if he don't cut his grass. He waited until I couldn't do it, then he cut his grass and called Pride about our weeds, the son of a bitch."

"Tom-tom," I said.

"OK, I'm hanging up," he said, and in his low, melodious voice, the one he always used on my mother, he added, "Oh, it's so good, man, to have you back here where you belong."

And he hung up.

I didn't unpack. He'd left me weak with irritability, he had interrupted my stride. I went out to the porch and sat claiming my territory, but I did not let my gaze stray beyond the veranda. Let the neighbors see me. But don't let them make eye contact. It won't make them less curious, but it keeps them from coming over. Some residual Spanish code of manners still operates in these Latin streets in Tampa. I believe this. That's one more reason I left New York. I was testing my block now. Could I sit on the porch whenever I wanted and not be bothered? There had once been a wooden swing at the end where I now sat. Shaded by a palm tree, and I had lain on it much of the time when I was a kid, after I gave up softball for reading. My mother and sister and grandfather spent the day at the factory (my father had died on me when I was seven) and no one bothered me then. Bother, it's a word I use a lot. But everyone on the block had seen me read. (And reach into my pants now and then to jerk off?) I know this from my first visit back years later when my mother took me round to her friends on the block and told them I wrote books and they all said, "I am not surprised— how you used to read when you were a boy!" Maybe I'll do that again. Read, not make the rounds. Dickens. I could be another man who loved Dickens. I waited and still did not look up: if someone comes over, I will have to get out of Tampa. If not, I shall buy a swing, but not a wooden one: something softer for my old bones.

No one came over.

I must build a character for myself. A persona, as the phonies now say. If someone asks me, I could say I'm a former writer. A new category: former writer. I liked that kind of bitterness. No slobbering appeal for sympathy. It is a matter of fact—especially down here where everyone had retired. I looked up, ready to share the thought and, thank God, there was no one on the porch across the street. Corona, a widow and more ancient than I, lived there. My wit would be lost on her. If she had any, she would have changed her name. Former writer, I repeated to myself and a heavy stone rolled off my chest—an apt, wounding epithet always calms me.

*   *   *

Tom-tom woke me. My head had fallen forward willy-nilly. I
slept like old people on New York park benches, and like them I
came to with a start. In terror. Was I being mugged?

"I scared you," Tom-tom said.

Was he trying to provoke me?

"I'm too old for that," I said and looked him full in the face.
He looked like his father, Papa Leandro, and it made me dizzy.
The dizziness had nothing to do with illness, but it reminded
me of my medicines.

"I have to go inside first," I said.

"Wait, wait," he said. "This ain't New York. There's time for
everything. Let me look at you."

I looked at him too. Somewhere on Papa Leandro's side there
must have been some peasants from the north of Spain. As-
turians or Basques or maybe Galicians like my father, for he was
broad and gave the impression of squatness, of a stone wall
astride a field; his hips were as wide as his shoulders and his
length was in his body not his legs. Papa Leandro could shift all
that volume delicately, sinuously, in a rumba danced on a
dime. Not Tom-tom: his legs were only meant to hold him up,
two sticks stuck wide apart into his barrel of a body, and he was
too alert to surrender to any music.

"Can you still get it up?" he said.

He laughed and he tried to shift his green eyes about to look
wicked, an old maneuver of his, ending in a misdirected
Rudolph Valentino amorous squint.

"You don't have to answer that," he said. "And you don't
have to ask me either."

Then with a sigh of nostalgia exuding brotherly warmth and
spit he grabbed my arm. "Oh, Pinpin," he exclaimed.

I shook my arm away. I am practically a Wasp now. All this
Latin touching and importuning makes me nervous.

"I'll be right back," I said and got to the screen door before he
did. I heard it slam behind me and damn if his voice didn't

continue. He was talking to the neighbors, for Christ's sake. I could hear him from the second bedroom where my backpack (I was just like the kids these days about that: carry your life with you) lay on mother's old bed, filled with medicines—beta blockers, diuretics, Valiums, Dalmanes, digitalis, insulin, syringes, the whole caboodle. I could swallow any without water, but some left a bitter trail, and I went off to the kitchen hearing Tom-tom still talking to someone. They'd all be invading the old house any minute.

"Wait, wait," Tom-tom said close by and startled me again. I said over my shoulder, "I'm just getting some water."

He held me back with his heavy grip. "Let me see. Maybe you take the same thing I do." He mauled the backpack, moving his big hands inside it, and added, "The one I take is a pink tablet. That's blue, isn't it?"

"What do you take?" I asked.

"I told you, a pink pill. It has a line down the middle, a little groove. Yours doesn't."

He was looking at the Valium. "Too yellow," he said.

I swallowed the Inderal to keep him from inspecting it. Maybe I should take a Valium. Get me through dinner with him and Olivia. Tom-tom pulled out a syringe from the backpack. I took it from him, shook out a Valium quick, and snatched the backpack from him and zippered it up.

"You're going to sleep in here?" he said unperturbed. "Why don't you take their front bedroom with the big bed?"

"I haven't decided," I said, and popped the Valium in my mouth.

"For God's sake, take some water," he said. "Go. Get some." He followed me to the kitchen.

"Not from the faucet!" He opened the tall refrigerator. There was a plastic pitcher-container there filled with water. He knew which cabinet door to open for glasses. "Here," he said. "Marina told me she got things ready for you."

"I asked her to," I explained.

We bickered: he said, "I knew," and I replied, "Then you were aware I was coming."

"You could've asked me too," he said, "or just me only. Marina is OK in case of a funeral but otherwise she's a terrible gossip. You don't want everybody to know your business. And there are some who say that she wasn't exactly fair about how she distributed Celia and Cuco's things, you know. You coulda asked me about that too."

"Actually, she volunteered to get the house in order." Why was I explaining?

"Of course, of course," he said. "She would."

Good that I took the Valium. There are nerves that still coil up, tighter and tighter, more or less on their own, for I don't really care. No more than I cared when Cora finally died. Peace, peace. Nor did I care now about Tom-tom or what he insinuated Marina took from the old house.

"Water from the faucet can kill you," he grumbled when I didn't reply. "Did she call you or you call her?"

"I don't remember," I said.

"That's just like you," he said. "I told Olivia, Pinpin is an innocent."

"Tom-tom, I can't stay with you too long, I have to get back here and unpack."

"You said you were going to unpack. Why didn't you? I gave you time."

I took a deep breath. I did not believe in answering questions of that kind. Of any kind. That's why I was here, because I wasn't going to answer questions or even listen to them.

"What are you going to do about a car?" Tom-tom said.

"There are taxis," I said. "They'll come to the house."

"What are you trying to do—insult me? I mean, a car for your visit here. I tell you what—I'll take you around. You can't walk and take buses like the old days. You'll be mugged. They go for old men first, you know. Bang. You can't walk over to the

Spanish Club or any place on Seventh Avenue. Remember old
Gumersindo Gonzalez, they got him when he walked to the
corner mailbox . . ."

And so on and so on.

In the car Tom-tom announced he wasn't taking the freeway.
He wanted me to see what it was like now going across town
from Ybor City (the old Latin section) to West Tampa (the
other, almost equally old Latin section). He didn't fool me; I
knew that none of my old cousins ever drove on the freeway. At
first, because like good Latins they didn't take easily to new
things; now, because they were old and scared of cars going
fifty. Celia and Cuco were an exception and look what happened to them: squashed and killed instantly by a truck that lost
its brakes on the freeway.

"I know, I know," I said when he began about the old American homes on Nebraska. "Everything has deteriorated."

"You can't know this," he said while we waited for the light
at Nebraska. "Take a look, I don't want them to see me pointing."

There they were, the young black prostitutes. You know
them: they're in your town too, on the worn-out old avenues,
Ninth in New York, etc., sticking their shining supple legs into
the street, giving the youngsters behind the wheel hardons,
hooking only the aging. The young get it free now.

"Why don't you want them to see you pointing? They're no
shrinking violets."

Tom-tom nudged me. "Their pimps are Marielitos, every one
of them. Look."

I looked, to please him.

"You know, Cubans. They'll slit your throat."

On the porch and sidewalk at the corner rooming house were
the pimps. Or were they dealers? Both, probably. They stood in
poses that went with the desuetude of the house. The two-story

clapboard was faded and grimy, the yard bare sand and scraggly weeds; so neglected it looked like a stage set. Down to the ersatz lace curtains at a couple of windows, near black with filth, their ends in shreds. The other windows were cavernous black holes. I could see the corner of a sheetless mattress.

"Jesus, I wish the light would change," Tom-tom said.

I had seen those guys in the Parque Central in Old Havana on my last assignment there. The park with the Jose Martí statue on which some of our sailors had pissed while on a rum grand liberty. Before Fidel, of course. Maybe it was their brothers or cousins I'd seen. They were Cuban, in any case, and malevolent in a special Caribbean way. Slithery, a half-smile always turned on, evil male Mona Lisas.

If I died at their hands, my life would be an overworked metaphor. Or a late, bad Tennessee Williams play.

Tom-tom said, "That's what Fidel sent us."

You let ten years go by without publishing and nobody knows who you are and what you wrote. Tom-tom of course had read nothing I wrote, but he should've remembered I had even met Fidel. (My Cuba book was out of print, needless to say.) I had to go up to Boston two months earlier (unwillingly) to see the law firm that has been handling Cora's family's byzantine investments and trusts since . . . oh, 1776 very likely, and the young-old preppy took a glancing jab at Cuba and I let him have it for old time's sakes, for Fidel and Che and Haydée Santamaría. He took a second look at my Brooks suit and silk knit tie and I saw him wonder how I could so brazenly sail under false colors. Then he remembered that I had not been born into Cora's family, that every generation suffers some defection in old Massachusetts Bay Colony families, et cetera.

God, I hate those Wasps now. Jews, too, the whole lot.

"You wanted them here," I said. "Come, come, to the land of freedom—so they came."

"Me?" he said. "Never." But he kept his voice low. "How

can you say that! If only in memory of my Papa Leandro."

He chuckled nostalgically. I didn't join him. I wasn't going to be sentimental about anybody.

"You know they threw red paint at our old house. Papa Leandro used to turn on the Havana station so loud when Fidel spoke that the whole block might as well have been at the meeting in Havana."

In his special adoring tone, he added, "And Aunt Mama, she was that way too."

"OK, OK," I said.

After a slight pause, for effect I swear—they're all actors in my family—he prodded me with his elbow. "Remember when we were young in New York? I was practically a Communist, right? And you weren't far behind."

"I *was* a Communist, you know that," I said. (What did he want?) "The Young Communist League."

He lowered his voice. "I didn't want to be the one to say it first."

"Why not?"

"It's very bad again. Anybody asks me, I tell them I voted for Reagan both times. I can't afford to be as crazy as Papa Leandro."

"Fuck 'em."

"What?"

"Tell them to take this fucking country and stick it up their asses."

He prodded me on the side again. "You're not going to talk that way around here, are you?"

"Why not? That's the way our parents and grandparents talked, remember?"

He lifted his eyebrows and moved his haunches.

"Didn't they?" I said.

"Yeah, but they're all dead."

And there's nobody to protect me. No uncle or older cousin

to stand on the porch and yell at the bully who's holding me down in the dirt.

That's not true about my uncles. They watched and said nothing. Later, when the fight was over, they would say, "You don't start it, but you hit back hard. And dirty. Anywhere you can reach him and give it all you've got. If you lose, don't cry. No tears."

No tears. Reagan is no more than we deserve. It's a dumb-ass country.

Don't start it—that's what I never could learn. Chin out, I attack, I insult, I yell—the old picket-line tactics. I had to learn, after I began to meet writers and publishing types, to correct idiots only with a Century Club hauteur. I stopped yelling; still, I stood my ground. But I never won. You could say I barged into things, but I spoke my piece coolly. I stayed awake nights turning the day over in my mind, rewriting the rejoinders I had made, getting ready for the next encounter, making resolutions—getting out of bed, finally, for a sleeping pill.

A couple of times a year we went up to Boston, more often as Cora grew older. (I think I grew less older than Cora and the rest of my generation.) I spent many an hour with her father or brother or cousin or old beau nodding about sailing in Maine or politely answering questions about my work as if reporting on a far-off exotic country. Then I would intentionally say something about something that I cared about—Martin Luther King, *Portnoy's Complaint*, Jules Feiffer, you name it—and they would respond:

"Yes, so I've heard."

Or, "Hmnnn—you believe that?"

Or, "Well, I shall have to look into that."

Or, "Old Tonky's on the board of United Fruit. It'll be fun to throw that his way and see how he gnaws on it."

Or, "How about more scotch?"

I hate scotch.

I had not counted on finding Cuban refugees in Tampa. I'd

have to think about that. I asked Tom-tom if there were any on my block.

"Oooh, they're all over! They're getting welfare, they're taking over the grocery stores, the drugs, they got everything now, man. My brother-in-law Serafin is involved with them. And Serafin has never been involved with anybody good."

"So they're accepted?"

"What do you mean?"

"People like them? They've made friends?"

"Me, I don't like them. Olivia won't even go into any store or restaurant they own." He laughed. "She says they make her want to scratch more."

"What's the matter with Olivia?"

"Some little thing, down there . . . women."

There was something else on his mind, and his face took on that serious air and his voice the dark tone that is sometimes genuine with him: "And then there is Papa Leandro and Aunt Mama and our Cuban grandfather and his Jose Martì this and Jose Martì that to take into consideration. It's bad luck to go against them too much."

I made a skeptical noise and wondered whether I really could live down here. Cuban refugees. *Gusanos.* Worms. The ghosts of our parents.

Tom-tom misunderstood and tried to head me off. "Now, Pinpin, don't yell at me about superstition and the hereafter. I don't believe in it any more than you do, but what if they're listening and watching and know if we're making friends with those counter-revolutionaries? That's what they would call them, you know—counter-revolutionaries."

His shoulders hunched over the wheel (his was some twelve-year-old American car, a Plymouth or a Dodge or something) but he decided to chuckle. He looked out the corners of his green eyes to see what I thought. He elbowed me again and said, "I was only fooling," but he only half was.

"I don't give a shit," I said.

"What! What! Didn't you—Aunt Mama said you used to go over there to Cuba to meet all the revolutionaries and write books. You wrote a whole book about it, right?"

"Where are we?" I said.

"Where are we?" he asked. "Oh, that's the bridge, we're crossing into West Tampa. Jesus, I don't have to tell you that's the Hillsborough River, do I?"

"It's all changed," I said, but I was thinking, it's all the same.

My sons came down here for two days when my mother died. Crispin drove to the funeral home alone with me once and on the way he said, "How do you tell one street corner from the other?"

He was right, but I still feel a residual cringe at his comment. His upper-class tone too, I guess.

"Well, I guess you're retired—you're sixty-five, right?" Tom-tom asked. Then added, "But you could always go back to it."

I liked that, so I said, "Maybe."

"Come on, you may get rusty but it's like everything else, right?" he said. He slowed down. "There's a little favor you can do me. You may have guessed. Let me tell you before we get to my place."

Here it comes.

"I need you to write a letter to the Traffic Department for me. About the Children Playing sign. The police won't do anything about it until they get a request from the Traffic Department, you see." He paused. "You're a writer, even if you're retired."

"That's the favor?"

"You can write it right on the typewriter without any mistakes. I want to mail it right off. I have a typewriter—someone wasn't paying the rent, you know—and that way they won't see any difference between the signature and the writing."

He elbowed me again. "You'll do it?"

I moved a bit away from him; it's not good for me to be

bruised. Hell, I forgot to transfer the insulin to the refrigerator. In Tampa it would boil and ferment in the backpack.

"That's what I was going to spend the evening doing—on my own birthday. Thinking of Aunt Mama too, of course. You were a professional, you can still zing off a letter, right? Will you do it, really?"

He lifted a hand off the wheel and poked my ribs. This time I moved to the window, and nodded. Was this all he wanted?

He slowed down even more. "Olivia has her own ideas how the letter should go. Yak, yak. A lot of boasting how we pay big taxes and that we own the apartment house. But I think we should go easy on that. Humility, that's the way to go."

"You cheating on taxes?"

"Ha, ha. But I don't want to give them ideas we should grease their palms. We gonna have to do it anyway, but there's no point raising their expectations. How do you like that—raising their expectations? That's very high-class English. You can make that letter as fancy as you like—but humble."

He speeded up again and we turned off Columbus into the dark little streets built after the war in those rattler-ridden scrub and palmettos of West Tampa. Golden real estate.

"Anyway, Olivia can't read any too well without glasses and she won't go out and get any with this scratching. So she won't put up an argument if you say you wrote what she said, more or less, right?" He chuckled. "First be humble, then if they're arrogant, knock em down."

"The police?"

"Them, never! The Traffic Department."

"What they taught us," I said and pointed at the roof of the car as he had done when talking about dead parents spying on us, "was to be polite. Humble is another matter."

"Have it your way. I'm ten years older, but you were always smarter. I got an empty apartment and that sign is a jinx. You gonna sell the old house? What do you want for it?"

So that was it.

"It's probably full of termites," he added.

I shook my head; he was bargaining.

"You're not?" He was thinking fast, speculating. "What you doing here?"

"I'm thinking . . ."

He went slower and slower, waiting for me to complete the sentence.

Finally, he said, "I didn't believe Marina. You know how she is—secretive, suspicious. You mean to live—"

"I'm thinking," I said. "I like to think in peace once in a while."

He swung the car slowly to the curb, muttered "fuck you" to the driver he cut off, and stopped altogether. There was a near-pileup of three cars, but he paid no attention to their honking.

"Tell me here now," he said. "I don't want Olivia interrupting when we get home. You say you're not selling the house and you're thinking of living here? For good?"

Goddamnit, I had told Marina, "I'm moving into the old house," at a moment when I had hit bottom and I was sorry I didn't take it back immediately. It was a kind of expletive and she should have understood. Not that I still didn't mean to stay. But I had to hedge: I didn't want all those cousins and the hundreds of children they had spawned breathing down my neck.

"I'm a little groggy from the plane and it's getting on to evening," I said. "Let's go on."

"But Marina practically said it outright."

"I'll ask Marina," I said. "Maybe she can tell me what I'm going to do."

"You're really coming back. I knew it, I knew it! You were the only holdout. Everybody came back, you know, when you could make a living again after the war in good old Tampa."

"But not in the cigar factories," I said, which to me were the palm trees in my garden of Eden.

"So what?" he said. "Who cares about the cigar factories, so what?" He stopped abruptly and pointed up. "Shush, they might be listening—Aunt Mama, my father." Then he took a deep breath and laughed.

So what?

That's my life— so what?

My hometown—gone.

My books—out of print.

Two sons—neither looks like me or thinks like me or—

Well, they're writers, I admit. I must have influenced them somehow. A role model, as they say without cringing at the jargon. Writers, but can you call living in Hollywood and dictating to secretaries writing? The characters and ideas in their scripts are so manhandled by agents, directors, producers, studio vice-presidents, and stars that only God knows who thought up what. Neither Crispin nor Jared owns a pen, I believe, or a typewriter or a notebook. When the secretaries aren't around they tap words into a word processor and it is equipped with a screenplay software floppy disk (get that?) that makes all the proper indentations and spacings and remembers the characters' names and tells the printer how to format (get that verb?) the whole thing into what looks like a perfect, finished script. They don't even have to know how to spell correctly (and they don't, having gone to all those progessive schools)—another floppy disk does that for them. From their separate homes the computers talk to one another, hill to beach, studio to yacht, Beverly Hills restaurant to Vegas casino.

Perhaps if I owned a computer they might talk to me too.

My one pleasure in this: their writing careers gall Aunt Snooky and Aunt Lucretia and Uncles Binky, Dinky, and Boo. These Boston idiots believe that real writers are venerable in their lifetimes, like Emerson, Longfellow, and Lowell. Still, the Hollywood grandnephews remain in their wills and codicils, and Cora's long last will and testament was a miracle of exclusion, adhering strictly to the royal line.

The things that Cora and I acquired together are mine for the damn little bit of life she left me to myself. (I think of myself now as having been an attendant prince. What a laugh, that flat-assed antelope a queen!) There's the furniture and paintings in the New York apartment, the books I bought on Fourth Avenue, the used linens, et cetera et cetera. But not the family silver nor the china service that they indeed ordered from China two and a half centuries ago, nor the Madeira tablecloths and the eighteen-by-thirty silk Kirman. Nor, of course, Aunt Harriet's Georgian house in Castine with half a mile of deep-water frontage. Mine—my very own—is the unheated house on the treeless hill in the midst of blueberry barrens where on a windy day you can get blown down running to the outhouse. It was my own writing studio in the days when, as the therapists say, I functioned. I bought it for two thousand one hundred dollars from a debased, holy-roller descendant of the great Puritans of the Massachusetts Bay Colony.

All the stuff in the New York apartment will probably be rejected by the Salvation Army and Goodwill on my death. They will sit in a clump on a sidewalk in the Village and perhaps the world's most assiduous scavengers will shelter them for a while. The house on the blueberry barrens will fall down and the boys will sell the land without taking a last look. My surname will suffer the fate of other Iberian ones that sneaked into New England—Fenollosa, Benét—no longer pronounceable in Spanish.

Mine shall end up as a game name. Computer games are all that interest my grandchildren, not stories, not books.

Anybody for Dos Passos?

Anybody for Santayana?

Nobody.

Tom-tom took two turns around his block before stopping at the house. Mostly because there was a car in his drive he didn't expect. "This ruins everything," he muttered. "I got to think it over."

"Take me home," I said.

"It's my sister Lila," he said. "Ralph used to keep her home and calm and then he went and died and she started going to old folks' dances."

"Lila," I said. "I like her."

"Watch out," he warned. "Ralph had more money put away than she thought and she got herself a facelift. In our family, a facelift! Now she tries to deny it, but I remember when she told me all, in a moment of weakness. I don't forget. Anyway, watch out for her."

He parked at the far end of the short block, under an oak tree alongside his apartment building. It was only a two-story stucco structure. Eight apartments at most. Dim lights inside and out. Very small rooms, most likely. His own home stood by itself at the corner we passed twice, facing away from the bastard-Bauhaus stucco. Between his kitchen and the back entrance of the apartments a garage-utility room intervened. Tom-tom turned in his seat, as much as the steering wheel and his paunch allowed, and looked back squinting and slowly shaking his head at Lila's car.

"I want an understanding before we go in there," he said sternly, waving a hand and pointing with the thumb.

"Who're you?" I said. "A Western sheriff?"

"Now listen, and no fooling," he said. "We don't have to worry about him. It's Lila who catches on fast."

"I thought you said he was dead," I said.

"Oh, Lila married again. You really been away too long. Some American who retired here. She caught him the first dance he went to. No money. A union pension and Social Security. He's dumb, he's from New Jersey. Lila tells him everything and he does it."

"OK, I won't worry about him," I said, but he didn't laugh.

"He's always smiling. You say something and he says what

can I tell you. Always. He's not asking. What can I tell you, that's all he says. It's no proper way to speak."

He lifted a hand and rubbed it over his face as if he were sopping up sweat with a towel. "I think Lila married him so she wouldn't have to mow the lawn. She lost both breasts like Mrs. Rockefeller and it was hard for her pushing the mower. Ralph wasn't a very active man—he used to sit on the porch and tell her what to do."

"Tom-tom," I said. "I've got to get back to my house."

"Your house?"

"Cuco and Celia's house, my house now."

"You're not selling, huh?"

I threw up my hands.

"I'm thinking, I'm thinking," he protested. He held my shoulder with his fleshy hand, his head with the other. "I'm trying to protect you too."

"Me?"

"First of all, not a word about Junior."

"Junior?" I said. "Who's Junior?"

"Jesus, that's a shock!" he said. "You don't remember my Junior? My only child? He used to shine your shoes in New York when you came out of the navy. You gave him money— he never forgot you and you don't remember him?"

"Sure, sure," I said. "I'm tired, that's all."

Tom-tom lowered his voice to what he considered an intimate, between-you-and-me level. "He was always a little backward, poor boy. Olivia's big worry, the cause of all her problems, though I always told her, he's all right, he's just a little backward. And I *am* right, he's OK."

A little backward? He was mentally retarded. If they had stayed in New York he might have tried for a job as a messenger, one of those you see midtown, staring at elevator push buttons trying to figure out what happened to number thirteen. Junior must be middle-aged now.

"You gave him all your navy shit—the kerchief, the little

white hats, the hammock. He loved you. He still asks about you every time we go to Miami."

"OK, OK, I remember him," I said. "I used to call him Jaime, not Junior. I still don't like that appellation. What's a Latin doing calling his son Junior?"

I put a hand on the car door and unlocked it and stretched a leg out towards the curb. He grabbed and pulled.

"Wait, yes, you're right. I'm sorry. You always had that craziness—I didn't mean that. I mean, you didn't want us to turn into regular Americans. Right?"

He was right; I was insane in those days. "Obsessed," I said, and nodded. Oh God.

"As if I could forget," Tom-tom said, pressing his advantage. "You and I, we're Tampa Latins. There's nothing we can do about that, but our children . . ."

"OK, OK. What about him? What's he doing in Miami?"

"Oh Pinpin, Junior is great. I think he's going to really do well with this wife. She works, she's one of those career women, women's liberation and all that and more, and he takes care of the condominium outdoors. And he does a few yards, mows lawns and things. In his neighborhood. Where he can walk over, because they won't give him a driver's license. It's very unfair."

"How come he's in Miami?"

"She got a job there in a bank and the other wife with the girls was in Tampa then, and we thought—well, I pointed out to Olivia that maybe the other marriages didn't work out because she and I were too involved, as they say. You know."

"What other marriages? Junior has been married more than once?"

"Five times," Tom-tom said, so low he was almost inaudible. Then he chuckled.

I brought my leg back into the car. "What's he got—a big wang?"

Tom-tom leaned over and put an arm around my shoulders,

squeezed and chuckled some more. "Oh Pinpin, he's always been a lovable boy."

"I bet."

"I used to pry him loose from his mother," he said. "You think . . .?"

"What are you saying?"

He pushed me away with his big meaty hands, then grabbed me back again. I felt like an uncooked hamburger.

"Jesus Christ, Pinpin," Tom-tom said. "I'm talking about psychology."

"So was I."

Tom-tom asked in his insinuating voice, "You think he's oversexed?"

I waited.

"Nowadays they say there's such a thing," he said.

I thought, maybe nature compensated down there for what it robbed him above, but said nothing.

Tom-tom grabbed me again. "Remember, say nothing about this inside. I don't mean—Jesus, Pinpin, you make me sound foolish."

I got out of the car and despite his bulk he ran around his side and caught up with me under the oak tree.

"Anyway, don't ask about Junior. And forget about his children. Yes, especially his children. OK?"

I nodded.

"And don't be surprised what you hear about the apartments. Lila don't know we own them. They think I'm the janitor, that's all. OK, let's go. On guard."

How did I get into this? I wasn't even hungry, and when I was, I was mighty finicky about what I ate.

He leaned on me as we walked and stopped me when we got to Lila's car. "I forgot, say nothing about the letter to the Traffic Department. I'll think of something to get rid of them and then you'll write the letter. We gotta wait them out, remember that. Wait them out, don't lose patience."

"Whataya talking about?" I said.

"It's Lila I worry about, not Conrad," he said and pulled me ahead as if I too were a burden.

"Conrad her husband's name?"

"Conrad Dupee. Isn't that ridiculous?" He stooped and looked at the back of Lila's car. "Dew-pee! It don't sound decent. And the dope hasn't done nothing about his muffler. He probably didn't get permission from Lila."

On the neat brick walk to his front door, Tom-tom threw his arm round me once more. It was exhausting.

"Oh Pinpin, if you only knew how glad I am that you are here. I need a real close relative like you to advise me."

The old seducer.

"I can't trust the others," he explained.

Don't trust me, I started to say, but reminded myself he didn't.

He thought of one more thing before we reached his door. "What's that word appellation? Be careful you don't make the letter too hard to read. They're a bunch of crackers at the Traffic Department. Worse, they may be Latins."

Two strange old ladies shrieked the moment Tom-tom opened the screen door and half-propelled me inside. They sprang from their seats. I halted and fell back into Tom-tom. Automatically, I brought up an arm to ward off their attack. Their faces lunged at me; enlarged, distorted, askew atop withering bodies. Deep wrinkles, blue-green mascara, painted eyebrows; agitated shrunken flesh on toothpick flailing arms; voices like the spurting, burping alarms of the emergency ambulances on the way to St. Vincent's in the Village.

"Pinpin! Pinpin!"

"It's Pinpin! Pinpin, how come?"

My cousin Lila wore the heavy mascara. "Aiee!" she went on, yelling and pushing Tom-tom's Olivia out of her way. "I didn't know. They didn't tell me!"

Olivia was taller and stuck her head towards me over Lila's shoulder. "I wanted to surprise her and instead I surprised myself! Pinpin, are you hungry?"

I felt the smeary contact of lipsticked kisses.

Lila screamed. "He's eating here! Why didn't you let me know, Pinpin? How long have you been in Tampa?"

A short, red-faced, blotchy, bald man stood carefully away from the two women and smiled as if he wished to be nearer: a satellite if ever I saw one. He was all plaid—shirt, pants, windbreaker.

"That's what happens if you live in Bradenton," Lila said to him, her wide mouth stretching and puckering four inches from my face, a considerable feat. "Did you know I live in Bradenton? When did I last see you? Oh, oh!" She threw both arms about my shoulders and hugged me against very firm B cups. "Celia! Cuco! What a tragedy!"

"He wasn't here when they died," Tom-tom said and pulled her away. "And you weren't at the funeral either, so don't make believe you saw him there."

"That's what I mean about Bradenton, it's too far away," Lila said. "You don't hear about anything."

Olivia tapped Lila on the shoulder. "Tom-tom called Pinpin right away and was the first, the very first, to welcome him home. I told him, Tom-tom call your Aunt Mama's house, I have a feeling . . ."

"Me too, me too," Lila said. "That's why we're out—I told Conrad—oh!"

She grabbed me by the wrist and pulled me towards the funny little plaid man. "Pinpin, I want you to meet Conrad. Conrad Dupee. My husband!"

Conrad started to bring a hand forward and so did I, but we both stopped and pulled back, as if short-circuited, when we heard Lila scream. I looked at her and saw in the midst of the parallel furrows of her face that her mouth was open in delight and that her shrieks were happy ones; it did not relax me.

"Look at him, look at him!" she yelled at me and pointed at Conrad. "Imagine me married to a man named Conrad!"

She doubled up, head down, and her yelps of laughter bounced off the floor.

"I'm all right, I'm all right," she said and straightened up. "I like a good laugh."

With that Conrad and I finally shook hands. Conrad was undisturbed, for Lila immediately placed an arm around him and her face next to his as if posing for a close-up portrait.

Conrad said, "What can I tell ya," and Tom-tom slapped me on the back as if to say I told you so.

"I'm Misses Conrad Dupee," Lila said, "and no cracks about going to the bathroom. Ha-ha, I'm only fooling."

Olivia said, "Pinpin, how did you find the old house? I can come over—"

Lila interrupted. "You see, you see, that's why we have to get out of Bradenton. We can't help anybody, we don't know what's happening—"

Tom-tom said, "Pinpin's got us."

"Yes," Olivia said quickly. "You've got your daughter in Bradenton—she needs you."

Lila exhaled a sigh full of spit. "Olivia, Olivia," she pleaded, "you know the situation there." She made a grimace at me that counted on my understanding. "We have discussed and you agreed. I've discussed with all my brothers and my sisters too. They agree. Except Sarita."

With a prod, Tom-tom led me towards the couch, but Lila wheeled and took my arm again. "You can't imagine what a bitch Sarita turned out to be. You remember her and her ways, I'm sure. I bet you've got a story or two to tell about her. I never realized it until it was as plain as the nose on my face. Then everyone in the family began to tell me about her but meanwhile she still owes me—I won't tell you how much. I'm an innocent, that's the kind of person I am. Conrad says so."

Tom-tom pushed her arm away. "He's gotta sit. He just arrived." He gave her a firmer push to dislodge her and prodded me towards the sofa once more. Its fabric was nubby and its innards hard as cement. "Let him rest before he eats."

"Of course, of course," Lila said and sat sideways on the couch in order to face me. "Pinpin, you look wonderful."

"As compared to when?" I said.

"He got you there!" Olivia said, and with the forefinger and thumb of each hand she held her loose cotton dress away from her body. "Haw, haw, haw!"

Lila smiled along with her. "As compared to always. I've known him always!" she screamed and leaned forward and I saw her wrinkles stretch like a bowstring and her mouth open wide for another machine-gun laugh. It bounced off the side of my face leaving it (eyeball included) paralyzed forever, like that of a stroke victim.

Olivia stood with legs apart and fanned herself with the skirt of her dress. "I can't scratch," she explained. "That's how many years we haven't seen you." She waved the dress obscenely. "Fungus! Ever heard of it?"

Lila caressed my arm. "Years and years, but you were always the handsome one in the family, that was my belief and it still is. Let the years go by, they don't bother you."

"Olivia!" Tom-tom called impatiently.

"Everything's all prepared," Olivia replied. "Give Pinpin a drink if you can get through," and gave Lila a glare as if she were a double-parked car.

"Listen, Pinpin," Lila said as soon as Tom-tom moved away from me, "if you want to keep the old house for old times' sake—you know, as a memento—keep it. Don't deny yourself the pleasure. Conrad and me are willing to live in it and take care of it for you."

"What can I tell you," Conrad said.

Tom-tom returned fast with a drink.

"Let's not give him any advice now," Tom-tom said. Then he gave Conrad and Lila what he considered his sly, disarming smile. "Let him have a drink and take it easy. He came over here because he wanted to take it easy."

Lila gave another liquefied sigh. Olivia directed one more disgusted look her way and left for the kitchen. Who would have thought they'd be so interested in me? It was hell.

"A house has to be lived in or it runs down," Lila said, quoting from her book of life. "I told Pinpin that Conrad and me would live in his house if he wants us to, because a house runs down—"

"Depends on who lives in it. Some people are worse for them than termites," Tom-tom said and gave her no chance to answer. He grabbed my arm. "How's the drink, little cousin?"

I nodded. It was ghastly. So sweet with rum and ginger ale and sugar and a maraschino cherry that I might have to take a couple of extra units of insulin tomorrow morning.

"Another cherry?" Tom-tom asked. "Ha-ha!"

Lila didn't get it. "Yeah, yeah," she said. "Give him another, Tom-tom. Don't you love them, Pinpin?"

Olivia stood before me with a plate of deep-fried green plantains. Like the drink, it was offered only to me. I looked at them and nodded and then at her and smiled. Any hostess at the hundreds of parties I have gone to in my wasted life would have passed on and let me be. Not Olivia. She remained there holding out the Bakelite dinner plate with its brickpile of bilious green plantains.

My mother used to slice them very thin on a small wooden contraption that looked like a planer for food. She deep-fried them fast and then shook them inside a paper bag to tamp the oil off them, and with a careful flick of her wrist lightly salted them. Divine.

But that was my mother, who required no Oedipus complex

to inspire admiration. Olivia obviously cut the plantain thick and then squashed the heavy slices with the heel of her hand and let them cook forever in shallow oil used for the hundredth time. *Tostones*, the Puerto Ricans call them.

(I must watch this superciliousness towards Puerto Ricans common in my family. They're no worse than anyone else and that's bad enough. No, fuck the Puerto Ricans too.)

I picked one up and felt the lard seeping through the pores of my forefinger and thumb. Rancid. I did not have to bite into it to know, but I did and confirmed it. My palate shrank. The plantain was lukewarm and the center raw and dry. It dropped to my stomach like dead weight. And yet there was a moment— fleeting, to be sure—when my body remembered happiness.

Olivia did not move away. She wanted me to take a second one immediately and I wished she would get the itch.

"Get him a napkin!" Lila said and jumped up and ran to the kitchen and back. "Here," she said and placed it on my knee and so rattled Olivia that she managed to take one of the *tostones* and bite into it before Olivia thought to move the dish out of her reach. "Delicious!" Lila shrieked and pushed my elbow and added, "Take another! Take another!"

Who would have thought there was so much agility in old Lila?

"Pinpin, don't get the idea that Lila cooked them," Tom-tom said. "Olivia made them—she's the champion of West Tampa."

Lila laughed and shrieked at that, slapping me and Tom-tom good-humoredly and waving the other arm at Olivia and Conrad as if asking them to join in on the joke.

Olivia jumped back. "Be careful," she said.

"That's right," Lila said, and not yet having withdrawn her outstretched hand took another plantain and held it out to Conrad. "Here, here, you yankee."

Conrad shrugged and took it, but did not say what can I tell you. He bit into it without changing expression.

Lila confided to me without lowering her voice that Conrad loved plantains, green or ripe. "But I have no time to cook them, we'd never get out of the house if I did. We have to drive far to visit—Bradenton is dead, forget it."

She turned to Olivia. "And what for? The TV dinners are better than anything any amateur cook can make. Right, Conrad? Don't you agree, Pinpin? And Pinpin has eaten everywhere, I bet. Why bother?"

Olivia handed the plate to Tom-tom. "Well, Pinpin, I don't have a TV dinner for you," she said in a sarcastically apologetic tone, and signaled to me to get up. "It's only *palomillo* steak and—"

"Oh, oh, I got to see this," Lila said, and headed for the kitchen ahead of everyone.

There was a formal dining table and six chairs at one end of the small living room, but you only ate there on Christmas Eve. Even the Nobel Prize would not have gotten me a place at that table on any other day of the year. I was being led to the kitchen.

I had managed to finish the first plantain, but held the other away from me.

Tom-tom said, "Eat up, there's plenty more," and like a fool I took a bite of it and felt my stomach trying to come up to meet it halfway.

"Where's the bathroom, please?" I said and headed for it, remembering that in Ybor City it is always behind the middle door of the three that give on directly to the living room. The bathroom is never demurely recessed at the end of a hallway; in fact, I didn't see a hallway in a home until I got to New York. Nor knew privacy, either.

"Right in there, right in there," Tom-tom said and didn't stop escorting me until I opened the door.

I quickly closed it behind me and sat on the edge of the bathtub next to the toilet. I threw the unfinished plantain into it and heard the others outside so clearly that I was sure the plop it made was audible to them.

Lila was saying, "You have to offer guests the bathroom. That's the first thing you do!"

I threw up into the toilet bowl as silently as I could manage, constricting my throat with an enormous effort, and then wiped the streams of oily acid at the edges of my mouth with purple toilet paper. I knew I could not survive this night.

Fourteen months since I last wrote prose. Ten years since I last published. Not a word in the last year, no journal entries, no letters, only checks to pay bills. Three months since Cora died—when I expected all my juices to start flowing again. That hope was years old, but I always suspected it would not work. You're checkmated if you're a writer: I knew the Dreiser story well, the one about the man who thought he'd be *free* when his wife died and, of course, was not. Look to literature for guidance, not life.

Here in Olivia's and Tom-tom's bathroom was the first time in a year that I missed the little notebook I once always carried in my shirt pocket. (Hard to find, stitched notebooks in that size; they're all spirals now and I hate them.) I missed my Mont Blanc, too, filled with Mont Blanc black ink. I wanted to start right then and there with a list of things I needed to buy if I was to stay in the old house. Or a list of alternatives to staying in Ybor City.

Let them forget me inside. Let Lila and Conrad Dupee leave for Bradenton without my good wishes. A short whiff of nausea rose to my tonsils and I leaned forward towards the bowl and wondered if I had also vomited the medicine I had taken at the house. Should I take more? What had I taken? I peered at my bile and lost my desire to vomit but not my queasiness.

Nowhere was now-here.

In the days when I was trying to puzzle out the English language by reading the *Tampa Tribune* (a loathsome newspaper), I was stuck for days with that one. You try to make now-here take the place of nowhere in the next sentence you run across it. I was eight years old. There was no point in asking my peers, and the grown-ups' English was no better than mine. (In Ybor City and West Tampa everyone spoke Spanish, even the Sicilians.) And anyway, I wanted to figure it out for myself. I cannot remember how I solved the mystery (probably because I don't want to give anyone credit; I'm not perfect) but now-here became the magic word, my own self-discovered mantra, that broke the spell of the worst obstacles, insuperable depressions, suicidal impulses.

Now-here, I said to myself (I never shared the magic word with anyone, not even with Cora after thirty-seven years of marriage and thirty-eight of cohabitation) and a little click took place and I knew that in a moment there would be light and, finally, even some hope.

It worked when:

(1) The first girl I took to the movies in New York slowly unbuttoned my fly and reached in with cool fingers and grabbed me and for a long minute of quivering fright nothing happened.

(2) Chamberlain went to Munich and I realized, squashed in the subway on the way to work, that the Spanish Republic could not hold out until . . .

(3) I had to bail out during my first gunnery training flight in Norfolk.

(4) Cora came out to the back porch of Aunt Harriet's house in Maine (by then Cora's) and saw Susie leaning back against a corner post in ecstasy, breathing in rhythm to my hand under her pleated Brooks skirt.

My mantra did not always work and such days were indeed black days. And the months, torture. It did not work when the articles began to be rejected and in time the books, after many rewrites, too. It didn't work in Tom-tom's bathroom.

Now-here was nowhere and vice-versa.

*   *   *

"Pinpin?" Tom-tom whispered and the sound came clear through those thin walls. "Pinpin?"

"Coming," I called.

"Does he have his own towel?" Lila asked.

"Use the pink one, Pinpin," Olivia yelled. "The pink one is always for guests."

Tom-tom opened the door slightly, only enough to look in and yet keep the others out of sight. "You OK? There's a pink towel by the washbasin."

"OK," I said and started to rinse my hands.

"Listen," he said in a lower voice, and slipped in and closed the door behind him, never letting go of the inside knob and pushing against it to keep Lila out. A remarkable maneuver for someone his size.

He walked towards me, but he could not quite reach me so long as he clung to the doorknob. He did not believe that he could not get as close as he wanted and he tried standing sideways and spreading his legs. No use. Finally, he pulled me toward him with his outstretched free hand.

He opened his eyes wide and looked desperate. He said, "I'm going crazy—stick with me tonight. Wait them out. Watch out for her intrigues."

I nodded towards the door to warn him that he could be heard, but he shook his head and continued. Olivia was making such a racket—had he signaled her to do so?—that he could have drowned me in the washbasin with no one the wiser.

"They'll want to drive you home," he hissed. "You say no."

"Maybe it's better for you—"

"No, no, I'm won't let her," he said loud. Then lowered his voice again. "She wants Celia's sewing machine—they'll put it in their car and haul off for Bradenton. You'll never see it again. They're scavengers!"

What the hell did I care? I shrugged.

"Actually, I know it for a fact, she said last week that she was going to write you. But of course she can't write and Conrad can't even make an X. She tried first with Marina, telling her you wouldn't miss it. Marina discussed it with me, they all depend on me—that's why I didn't tell Lila you were coming. I'm doing my best to protect you."

"It doesn't matter," I said.

Tom-tom leaned against me and grabbed me by the back of my neck. He looked aghast. "What doesn't matter?"

"I don't know," I said. "I want you to take me home. Lila talks too loud and I'm tired."

He was very relieved. "Yes, she's uncivilized," he said. "We'll have a quiet talk as soon as I get rid of her."

He got me out of the bathroom and into the kitchen without my being able to explain that I wanted to be taken home right away. I was sure I had vomited the medicines; I needed to think; I had to lie down. I searched my pockets; no medicines.

How came I at an age when Social Security, in all its forms, including the monthly paycheck, should be my lot and reward—how came I to be sitting in this tacky kitchen, wedged in between a hot stove and a white-enameled table that predated Formica, surrounded by ghoulish reincarnations of my childhood, when I had known since the age of ten that I was meant for New York and literature?

That is the question, I said to myself, and jumped and banged against the noisy table when the phone stuck to the wall next to my ear rang piercingly.

"*That* is loud!" Lila said at a considerably higher decibel level.

"Tom-tom fixed it," Olivia said, "so he could hear it out in the yard."

I was better prepared for the second ring.

"Shush," Tom-tom said to everyone. He picked up the phone and said cautiously, "Hello." He narrowed his eyes. "A little louder, please."

Olivia announced, "I'm not serving until he's off that phone—it is too distracting."

I nodded and covered the ear nearest the phone with one hand.

"Who is it?" Lila asked. "If it's one of my sisters, I want to talk to her."

"Oh, Marina," Tom-tom said, "it's you, how nice."

Lila said, "I want to talk to her."

So did I, but I no longer felt I could influence the course of events while Tom-tom was in charge and the others around. I should have called her as soon as I arrived. I had questions about the old house. She might be helpful without being sticky. Get me a yardman and a housecleaner—I still hate to say maid; some proletarian heritage, that.

I lifted a hand to Tom-tom to indicate he should hand me the phone when he was done.

"Yes, there're people here," he said. "Maybe—"

Lila screamed, "It's Lila, Lila!"

"Maybe I can call you tomorrow, because now . . ." His face took on a wary look, his eyes darted to Olivia, then to me. "They saw Pinpin sitting on the porch?"

Marina was closing in on him. She had been librarian of the Ybor City branch, and no one in the state had a better record than she in lost books.

"Well, they ruined my surprise, Marina. Pinpin came over to have dinner with us—you know how close we've always been—and I was going to put him on the phone to you as soon as he finished," he said, not relinquishing it yet. "Maybe you should talk to him later or tomorrow—that way he can eat in peace?"

Lila let go her machine-gun laugh.

Tom-tom frowned. "He's still eating. Well, all right."

He finally let me have the phone.

I did not get to say hello. Marina spoke in a fast whisper, in what no doubt was her professional voice, though she had retired at least a decade ago. It had, like the voice of all librarians, a sweet edge to it that lacked, as the literary critics say, sincerity.

"This is not a proper hello, and I hope you hear me *clearly* Pinpin, because I don't want to *raise* my voice. You can imagine *why*. They mean to *clean* you out. *He* has laid siege for *weeks* and *she* too. There's *nothing* they don't want. Be careful how you answer questions. *He* rents a table at the flea market and he's *always* looking for merchandise. Anyway, be *on guard*. I'll come first thing tomorrow morning. Say yes to *nothing*. On guard, Pinpin!"

On guard: they all went in for the phrase. People grown old in a Nelson Eddy–Jeanette MacDonald operetta. I should reply in song, I thought . . .

And she hung up.

I never got to say anything. What did I want to say? Oh yes, I wanted to say thanks. But that's the way the world is, you can't even say thanks.

"I never got to talk to her!" Lila yelled.

Tom-tom stared hard at the phone, as if it might give up its secrets, then at me. "What'd she say?"

I shrugged. "Hello."

"She's a very sweet person, Marina is," Tom-tom said.

"Oh yes," Olivia said.

"That's what everybody says," Lila said.

A pause. Who would utter the first caveat?

(Why did I write that? I mean, the word *caveat*, this decade's trendy revival. The result of academics appearing on talk shows, yuppies watching PBS, outreach journalese.)

I could volunteer one about Marina: a librarian ought to have read more than *Gone with the Wind* to be trusted.

But we outwaited one another.

Conrad broke the silence with "What can I say," and I liked him for it.

Lila sat down at the kitchen table. "Nothing for me," she said to Olivia who simply stared back. "I'm just waiting for Pinpin to finish and then Conrad and I are driving him home."

"It's not on the way to Bradenton," Olivia said.

"We're out in the car already and it's less trouble than for Tom-tom who's getting old to take out his car and come and go, right Conrad?"

Conrad never got to say his line. Tom-tom waved an arm for silence and in a tone that made Lila's deep wrinkles come to rest said, "Pinpin and I have some business to talk over and he's tired and so you and Conrad had better come to visit another time and then we can all relax."

"OK, I understand," Lila said and she nodded three or four times, soberly thinking it all over, and then she got up and nodded again with resignation. She drummed her long, pink-lacquered nails on the metal top of the table. "Well, I guess I struck out this time," she said. She reached out and patted my shoulder. "See you soon, Pinpin."

Olivia served the *palomillo* steaks. Tom-tom sat down between me and Lila's end of the table, somewhat relieved at Lila's resignation, though his face announced that there was still hard work ahead.

For one thing, Lila had not yet actually left. He looked at her. "See you then."

He turned to me. "Look at that, Pinpin, isn't that just like Aunt Mama used to make it?"

The *palomillo* steak was cut thin all right, thinner than it should've been, in fact; and this one curled at the edges like a worn shoe half-sole and the french fries sat in a limp mound on the side. The thin juicy slivers of pristine onion my mother scattered over the steak were represented in Olivia's version by second-hand yellowing hard slices.

Lila said in a defeated voice, "You forgot the slice of lemon."

"Oh, oh," Olivia said and from her seat in the tiny kitchen reached the refrigerator door, opened it, and retrieved half a lemon. "Here," she said, handing the dry relic to me.

Lila slapped her thighs and bent over in a sudden motion. She looked stricken. I tried to get up and I banged the table again and was forced to sit, but by then I could hear Lila's shrieking laughs and knew, if one could put it that way, that she was all right and had fooled me again.

Lila could not stop laughing. She'd call out my name each time she caught her breath and then go off in a series of shrieks. She put out a hand and Conrad placed a handkerchief in it without being asked and she tamped it alternately in the corners of her eyes.

Conrad stood in the doorway at peace, and Tom-tom and Olivia would not look her way.

When Lila got her breath back for good, she asked, "How's my mascara?" And without waiting for an answer made (I thought) her last try. "Pinpin, I'll come clean—I wanted to ask you, when we were alone and you could speak frankly, I wanted to ask you a favor. I didn't want to embarrass Tom-tom and Olivia by doing it in their home. That's why I wanted to drive you home. But you got to answer frankly, remember."

"Sure," I said and looked up at her and suddenly saw her face of old.

When I was a boy (five to eight?) and I could not read much more than the comics, Lila, who was as old as my sister Celia, would tell me stories. I used to ask everyone to tell me stories, I could not get enough, but only grandpa and Lila always responded. Weekends she came to the house to join Celia and my cousin Marina to go to the movies or wherever girls went and I'd wait for her on the porch and beg for a story. She would actually postpone going inside to Celia and sit on the swing with me and tell me stories. Stories, I later realized, that she picked up from *True Confessions*: loves lost, loves regained, infidelities, undying loyalties. And when she came to the end of each one she would make me look at her and she would say, "And so you see, everything came out all right." She didn't laugh or grin, and certainly never shrieked, when she said it, but looked at me as she did now: waiting benignly for my agreement. Gaiety was her rock-bottom despair.

"I was going to ask you if you're meaning to keep Celia's Singer sewing machine," she said.

"I—I—" I began, remembering Marina's admonitions.

"Please, please, don't say anything now!" She threw out an arm as if to block an entire football lineup. "No, no. Eat now. I'll talk to you another day when you've had a chance to put a price on it. Conrad wants to buy it as a present for me, isn't that sweet?"

"Listen, I—" I began again.

"Pinpin has practically already asked us to take such things off his hands," Tom-tom said without waiting to swallow his mouthful of steak and without, of course, looking at me.

I said cowardly, "Marina asked to speak to her about the house first."

Lila did not look at me, which was wonderfully tactful of her, nor at her brother nor Olivia. She drummed on the table again and said, "Well, Olivia, congratulations. Maybe you'll let me come over and use it before you start taking sewing lessons?"

"Why do you say that?" Olivia objected.

"You're not going to the public school classes to take lessons like Marina? Poor Marina, she will be so disappointed."

Olivia turned to Tom-tom. "You see, you see?"

Lila continued, "Or I can teach you if you got the time. I taught my daughter and that Mrs. Fisher in Bradenton. She already made herself—"

"Tom-tom, aren't you going to say anything?" Olivia said. "I know how to sew, thank you. It's that Marina who doesn't know a needle from her nose."

This time Tom-tom really could not open his mouth, it was so full.

I said, "Please forgive me, but I do want Lila to have the sewing machine."

They all stared at me. Conrad separated himself from the side of the door and looked frightened.

"For old times' sake," I added.

"That is what I call sweet," Lila said. "That really is. But I can't let you do it. No, no, no."

And so on and on it went. Shit, her moment of sincerity had been only a mirage visible to me alone, and here I was stuck with this awful food in this noisy restaurant. I moved the food around on the plate as if that might use it up. Tom-tom said something and then Lila and then Olivia and then Lila and Lila and Lila.

It took Lila some time to convince Olivia and Tom-tom that she would not accept the sewing machine from me. Not that either put up much of a fight to the idea, but I had said what I had said and they kept requiring confirmation from Lila. They referred to my offer over and over and Lila kept saying no, no.

Finally, Lila turned my way and practically sang an aria. Pure bel canto: "Pinpin, you should've seen how good Tom-tom and Olivia acted when Cuco and Celia, may they rest in peace, met with their awful tragedy. I was sick—you can ask my daughter—and could do nothing, but they took care of everything, everything. Some people may try to take credit at a time when you were coping with your own wife's health and could not come yourself and thus really know who was involved and who was not. But I know. I tell you honestly, Tom-tom and Olivia deserve your gratitude and—I might as well say it—your gifts."

At this point, she turned to Conrad and asked, "Conrad, if I died, wouldn't you turn to them and only them?"

Conrad knew better than to answer.

"When you were sorrowing for your own poor Nora, that's how good Tom-tom was—"

Olivia was agape, but Tom-tom interrupted, "Not Nora—Cora."

Lila emitted a scream and said, "How could I forget! Why, she spent most of your mother's funeral talking to me! Of course, Cora, of course."

She went on praising Tom-tom and Olivia and refusing the gift of the sewing machine long after there was no resistance to her suggestion. Only puzzlement.

Finally, she concluded, "I know they would come through for me too, if ever I needed them."

Olivia said, "Whatever we can do, Lila," and Tom-tom gave his wife a warning look.

Son of a bitch, none of them fooled me. Some maneuver was going on, I didn't know what and I didn't give a shit. I guess the food on my plate hardened me to them. I wasn't going to eat that piece of leather and throw up again.

I tried the french fries. No good. She had cooked them in the same oil as the plantains.

Then, when Olivia and Tom-tom (and me too) thought that she was really leaving, Lila dropped the bomb.

"I almost forgot," she said from the doorway to the living room. "It was such a surprise to see Pinpin—oh, Pinpin, we're going to call you before you go, when do you go?"

"I don't know," I said.

"Never mind, we'll get together," she said, and just then with Olivia and Tom-tom off guard, she said in the same quiet voice she had used to ask for the sewing machine, "That second-story apartment to the back is empty and Conrad and I want to rent it."

"I told you—" Tom-tom began.

"Three times this week we passed by," she interrupted, "and there was no lights. The venetian blinds are there but there is no curtains! No curtains!"

"They're away on a trip," Tom-tom said, and after a pause threw in, "I think."

Olivia said, "Yes, the neighbor told me."

Lila ignored her. She asked Tom-tom, "Did you speak to the agency?"

"What agency?" Olivia asked.

"The one that manages the building," Tom-tom hurried to say.

"There is no agency, tell the truth," Lila said. "No agency. I found out. I mean I found *you* out, big brother."

A terrible outcry from all three. Accusations and counter-accusations, but long before Tom-tom acknowledged or denied that he owned the apartments ("Who told you?" he kept asking, and Lila kept repeating, "That's for me to know and you to find out") I got rid of the steak and french fries in the garbage pail on the side of the stove. Even Conrad didn't notice me do it. He had retreated into the living room; the recriminations in the kitchen were joined by the sounds of a rerun of "Kojak" from the living room. Then Tom-tom decided to explain to Lila why she would be an undesirable tenant and neighbor and he drowned out everything else.

Much of the time Olivia backed up against the refrigerator and fanned her legs with the skirt of her loose cotton house-dress. "I'll have to scratch!" she warned. "I'll have to scratch!"

Lila listened to the bad character references Tom-tom was giving her and only occasionally a twitch flitted across her wrinkled face.

"You didn't get along with your husband, you don't get along with your daughter, and every cash register in Hillsborough County has a notice on it—do not accept checks from Lila Dupee a/k/a Lila Gomez a/k/a whatever name you used when you started not paying bills at the age of ten."

"You finished?" she asked.

"I should have you next door and be forced to go collect the rent from you every month? No thanks, nosiree. That's my job, you know, to collect rents. I should take on a headache like that, I'd have a heart attack too."

Who'd had a heart attack? I placed a hand over my heart. That's the middle of the chest, not the left side. Those disgusting lithographs of Jesus's flaming heart were right all along. Did Lila's former husband have a heart attack? What was his name? I thought, finally, of Cora dead white against the anarchist colors of the bedspread. What was I thinking of? She had died of cancer.

"And that's that," Tom-tom said. "And no more."

(How he continued to avoid the subject of the ownership of the apartments is too labyrinthine to recount.)

Lila took a deep breath. "First of all," she began, "my daughter loves me."

Desperate that there was more of the tirade still ahead, I picked up what was left of my drink. I had to have something— let it kill me. Let Lila rip.

To my surprise and Olivia's and Tom-tom's, Lila said no more. She swallowed hard a couple of times and took off, and Conrad had to run to turn off the TV to catch up with her. The rest of us got up and watched her from the kitchen door. At the front door she stopped and gave herself the once-over and perked up a flounce on her blouse and after calling to me, "Pin-pin, say hello to your children!" she walked out sedately with Conrad following. There were people outside looking, that's why she quieted down. Maybe.

I lifted my glass to her as farewell.

"Hi there, hi there," she said as soon as she stepped out, as if she were running for public office and the people on the sidewalk were her constituents.

"Oh my God, oh my God," Olivia said. She walked back into the kitchen looking like a turtle in her attempt to keep her legs from brushing against each other. "I'm going to make coffee now and we can just forget about everything."

I looked out the kitchen window and there were some people out on that sidewalk too. Not exactly a crowd staring at me staring at them, but they didn't just happen to be out walking either. I didn't know them and they didn't know me, but I had to get out of this or end up in some disturbance-of-the-peace mass arrest, the kind of news they report on minor New York TV stations and that down here is probably big news for the crackers and would surely be the end of my retreat into anonymity. What a mess for my biographers!

The screen door opened out front before we sat down and Lila stuck her head inside. "Olivia," she called, "don't forget to tell Tom-tom what I told you about Dulcie."

"Oh my God!" Olivia wailed, and Lila's face vanished before Olivia's wail turned into sobs.

Tom-tom jumped. "What about Dulcie?" He ran across the room but stopped at the screen door when he saw the people on the sidewalk. He too worried about his biographers.

My biographers! God, we are vain, we writers. We learn soon enough to live with humiliation, but we never accept rejection for ourselves, only for others; it is they who will turn into the nameless writers of worn, dull books sitting on the shelves of cheap maple breakfronts and cutesy dropleaf desks at wayside used-furniture stores whose owners would drop dead if anyone attempted to buy the books rather than the furniture. As for myself, of course I am going to have biographers; ambitious young scholars will write their theses on one aspect or the other of my work; and there will of necessity be a uniform edition of my complete works at which riper scholars will have labored, with the help of any number of grants, to restore the punctuation and syntax—indeed, the whole damn text that girl editors changed or excised.

Indubitably, it is not without interest, this life of mine. No, no, that way lies the beginning of another story or article or novel in the course of writing which I always inevitably came to feel that old self-love and unrealizable ambition that would cause me to phone Jared and Crispin . . .

"I'm holing up," I say, in that special, slightly nasal voice I cultivated up north. "Starting another novel. Can't keep a dog from its old runs."

"Well, that's grand, pop," Jared says.

"What's the title?" Crispin asks, being like his mother more skeptical, but showing, also like his mother, more interest.

These are the responses I get if their movie deals are breaking well at the moment. Followed by a chat and promises to call soon and their taking down my new work schedule and the titles of new novels I recommend, all abruptly ended by a call on another wire (oh, they have other wires, all right, all right, all right) or more likely by signals from a wife or lover who was not, definitely not, going to put up with the old bastard.

I hate women.

But if their deals are in turn-around and they are thinking of switching therapists or agents, Jared says, "They're your real grandchildren, pop, aren't they?" to remind me that once again I have failed to ask about his.

Crispin, to whom New England nasality comes naturally and who has no children: "I told them at lunch yesterday, I know some one to whom the written word comes first. God, who's that? Father, I told them."

I have called them only twice since my operation six years ago. They had phoned while I was in the hospital and I was so short of breath that I could barely reply. Jared sent flowers and wrote on the card—or had written for him, rather—that the current wife and their children sent love too. Crispin sent two jokey telegrams. In his name only: he never let the girls hang around long enough for them to acquire any status, often not even a name. But there were no calls from them the moment I was home and could speak at any length. OK, I said to myself, I can be as much of a Wasp as anybody.

Yet they kept in touch with Cora, and she sometimes put me on after her aseptic but entwining chats with them. If they

didn't call for a week, she didn't care. They came to her funeral, if you can call an unceremonial cremation a funeral, and
went up to Boston on their own to talk to the family lawyers *et
al.* I am not sure they will do anything in my case. Let some
agent handle it all for them.

I'll be leaving them damn little. Fifty percent of the proceeds
from my out-of-print books. What a laugh.

They came east for a week towards the end of Cora's illness
and we weren't doing badly together until one day, when I was
midtown and called home to say I'd be late, and inadvertently
heard the two of them on the phone. It was a kind of nightmare
error of the phone company's (maybe the result of all the taping
the FBI must do with Cora's continued activism) that I was
plugged into their conversation. Jared was at our apartment;
Crispin somewhere with some girl. It was the kind of thing that
happens in life but never in fiction.

I heard a laugh and Crispin say, "And dad?"

"He's not here," Jared said.

"Seeing his agent?" Crispin asked.

"God, I hope he gets an assignment," Jared said. "Aren't
there Third World troubles somewhere—"

Crispin cut him short. "He's out boffing Aunt Susie more
likely."

Jared exclaimed, "Jesus, you think that's still going on?"

His brother said, "Who do you think I got my gonads from?"

I put down the phone with murder in my heart.

What was I saying? Where was I?

I was wrong about Tom-tom. He didn't care about the neighbors;
he opened the screen door and bellowed, "Lila, come here!"

She came: there was no denying that voice. As she neared
him a choked rumbling noise came out of him. I caught the
name Dulcie and somehow knew in my daze that he did not
want me to.

"What's the matter?" she said. "You shouldn't get so upset at your age."

He stared at the people on the sidewalk as if they owed him rent. He did not speak again until Lila was inside and the people started moving away. All of which, given his bulk and consequent authority, happened quickly.

I watched. Was this the hardness at the hard core of him? I sat down; the sweet rum had gotten to me.

"Lila, now listen to this," Tom-tom said, and Lila knew him better than I did, for she did not cower but calmly waited. "You can have the apartment. Anytime, starting tomorrow, for I don't want to see you again tonight. The first month's rent in advance."

She jumped like a little girl, up and down, up and down, and got her arms around his neck on her third jump, a difficult position to maintain because his belly forced her feet slightly off the ground. She smeared lipstick on his cheek and then me too and laughed and rubbed off the traces plus those of her welcoming kisses of an hour ago. She started jumping again at Tom-tom to do the same for him, but this time he held her off.

"All right, all right," Tom-tom protested. "Just remember I did this for you, that's all."

"I knew it, I knew it!" Lila said. "You have such a big heart. I say so all the time, I don't care what enemies it makes me. Ha-ha! I'm kidding."

"The apartment is clean now," Tom-tom said.

"Spotless," Olivia said.

"And you'd better keep it that way," Tom-tom added.

"Isn't he good?" Lila said and turned to Olivia and then to me and repeated, "Isn't he good?"

Olivia burped.

"You'll see what a good choice you made," Lila said, stroking his arm and leaning her grinning skull on it. "We'll help you here. Conrad will mow the lawn—he'll keep up the yard for you. We won't bother you—I promise—but you can always count on us—"

She let go of Tom-tom and went towards Olivia. Olivia sat down with her legs spread wide, each foot on a separate ottoman. She said, "Don't jostle me, be careful."

"Oh, Olivia, I'll take you to the doctor, do the shopping for you—"

"No need for that," Tom-tom said.

Lila leaned over, however, and spoke into Olivia's face with many grimaces to make up for not touching her.

(In my family every idiot worries about being insufficiently expressive.)

"I mean that about the sewing," Lila said. "Anything I can do for you. You don't even have to learn, not from anybody— I'll sew whatever you need."

Olivia frowned. "I want the sewing machine here. As soon as I get rid of this thing I have I am going to do my own sewing, thank you."

"Of course, of course," Lila agreed.

She threw out her arms and turned from her to Tom-tom and back again and once or twice to me during her gyrations, with her arms outspread all the time and a taffy-pulling series of contortions exercising her wrinkles.

"It's not that my daughter doesn't love me," she said, and the grimaces stopped and genuine tears began to flow. "You just shouldn't move in with your married children. It's not like the old days. They don't expect to have mother-in-laws, you know, they are not supposed to exist."

She laughed but the tears did not stop.

"That's what I am. I am a nuisance. I'm a pain in the ass. Excuse the language, Pinpin, but that's the truth. It's not her fault, she's a good girl—and those wonderful children. I'm practically ruining her marriage."

She began to sob.

Olivia said, "Shit, you bought them the house—"

"Yes," Tom-tom said, "and Ralph didn't mean his insurance to go for that—it was for your old age."

Ralph, that was her husband's name. Rafael, actually: a stolid Latin of Galician descent.

"They going to pay you for that now?" Olivia said. "They shoulda least pay your rent."

"Oh no, oh no," Lila said happily. "Oh, everything's going to be all right now." She wiped her face with a handkerchief she extracted from her blouse and skipped to the door and looked out at her car where Conrad still waited for her. "Tom-tom, thank you." She wiped her face again and left it streaked with the colors of her makeup like a punk hairdo. "Wait till I tell Conrad!"

Tom-tom said, "What can I tell you."

Lila was the first to laugh—she always was—then Olivia, then Tom-tom at his own joke. What a hullaballoo! Even I laughed.

It was a mistake to have joined in the laughter. It took Tom-tom off the hook: he relaxed about taking me home right away. I'd die here.

"Conrad is really no problem," he said as soon as she was gone, stalling for time, getting ready, I thought, for bringing up my letter to the Traffic Department. "It's Lila—I hope she minds her own business."

Olivia said, "Those grandchildren are monsters and her daughter the less said the better."

Something occurred to Tom-tom and he half-stood and struck his head with one hand like a silent-movie actor. "I forgot!" He ran to the door, but Lila and Conrad were under way, their car's imperfect muffler supplying an unforgettable last farewell.

He pointed to Olivia and shook a finger, unable to talk. He exploded. "My God, I forgot!"

"What?" she said.

"What did she tell you about—" He looked at me and back at her. "What was it?"

"It was nothing," Olivia said. "I'll start the coffee again."

But she did not get up and she covered her face with both hands.

He yelled, "Dulcie!"

"Her daughter thought she saw her on Dale Mabry," Olivia said and covered her face again.

"Thought?"

"That's all—thought," Olivia replied and began to cry.

He took a hesitant step towards her. She emitted a sob, or burped, or something.

"That's all right, that's all right, sugar," he said in a soothing voice that sounded amorous.

(He knew only two approaches with women—amorousness and irritability.)

He placed a fat hand on her bony one. "Come on now, honey," he continued. "Do what your Tom-tom says. There's nothing to worry about. *Thought*. That's not a sure thing, like if they talked to her. You were right—we won't think about it, sweetheart."

With each word she breathed easier, until she looked around and said, "I'm going to make you that coffee."

I suppose I should have asked what that was all about, especially since Tom-tom didn't want me to know. But I didn't and didn't plan to—I wanted home.

Tom-tom brightened up. "I have a better idea. Pinpin is tired. I want to help him to—whatever. And you could use a rest yourself after cooking that dinner . . ."

She was not difficult to persuade. I got up immediately to show I wasn't eager to stay and, after all, I wasn't fun company for her.

"You don't mind, Pinpin?" she said.

"I have to unpack," I said, I think for the hundredth time since I got off the plane.

"Next time then, Pinpin," she said. "I'll make you a real meal and rice pudding like your mother used to make."

"Oh honey, you know I love you," Tom-tom said, "but nobody can make rice pudding like Aunt Mama. Nobody. If a month went by and she didn't make it, I'd call her up. Aunt Mama, I'd say, and she'd come right back—Tom-tom, you must want some rice pudding!"

And so on, the old mushmouth; to all our Latin kiss-your-ass courtesy he had added southern bullshit nostalgia. He was buttering me up for something, for sure. Something more than the letter to the Traffic Department.

"And we'll forget about the letter tonight, Pinpin," he said, as if he had read my thoughts. "Another day. Tonight I am content to listen to you talk. It's been so long. It's music to my ears. Remember when you first arrived in New York? Olivia was pregnant with Junior and I got you that job at the cafeteria?"

"As dishwasher," I said.

He slapped me on the back and laughed. "It was the Depression," he said. "There wasn't anything better." He held the door open and called, "So long, mama."

I waved at her too, and decided to stop suspecting Tom-tom of anything. There were no neighbors on the sidewalk; it had all been a passing Florida squall.

"Depression or not, I appreciated it," I said.

He exhaled good feeling and led me to the car with an arm around my shoulder.

"It's better to leave early," he half-whispered. "We'll have time for a good talk."

Oh, oh, this wasn't good.

He turned on the ignition and said, "What do you say we get you that coffee on Dale Mabry?"

"Well," I said.

"And maybe a little something to eat, too," he said. "I saw you throw away the food—that's why I got you out of the house, to feed you. Poor Olivia, she tries, but she's not Aunt Mama."

He left me no out. "I'm sorry," I said.

"You did me a favor," he said. "Let's go to McDonald's—"

"McDonald's?" God.

"You prefer Burger King?"

I didn't bother to answer that.

"Some people do, but not me. I'm still loyal to McDonald's. Burger King is just a bad copy. I love french fries, don't tell Olivia, and sometimes I sneak out—Dale Mabry is only five blocks away—and get a large order and eat them in the car. How do you think I got so fat!"

"OK," I said. I had never been in a McDonald's. The last holdout was turning into the OK Corral.

But Tom-tom caught my hesitation or lack of enthusiasm or distaste or all of them and as quick as an insurance salesman he stepped up his pitch. I remained glum. Why not? I no longer put a good face on things as I had been taught.

(Oh, I could deliver a lecture on how a Spanish upbringing disables you for life in these United States.)

And so, to keep me interested, he said, "Dale Mabry goes on growing, even more than when you were here the last time. I don't know where the money is coming from. How do you explain it, Pinpin?"

I didn't reply to that hokey make-talk either. I said, "That was very nice of you to let Lila have the apartment, Tom-tom."

"Have!" he genuinely exclaimed. "They're going to pay rent."

"That's what I meant."

He paused only a moment. "You didn't see my mother much during her last years. She didn't have that happy look like Aunt Mama, she got all wrinkled and nervous like Lila."

That sentimental I was not going to get: I would end up the perfect mark, giving him whatever it was he wanted from me.

"Here's Dale Mabry!" he announced. "Back there they opened a supermarket one block long. Pak It Yahself. The fish counter is half a block long. They got anything in the world you want and more. Open twenty-four hours a day. On the way back—"

"What way back?" I said.

"I mean, we'll stop there, so you can buy whatever you need for yourself at the house. OK?" he said in a voice that was almost amorous. "OK, Pinpin? You'll be needing things . . . if you stay?"

I let that pass too.

"Here we go," he said, and turned into Dale Mabry, a couple of miles of America: motels, hotels, fast-food chains of every kind, pet-grooming parlors, shopping centers, drive-in banks, landscaping centers, car washes, karate gyms. Tom-tom drove slowly along the outer lane going south, pointing out each one's specialty. "Video, video, that's the new thing. I guess you got one of those up in New York. You can watch dirty movies on them."

After a pause: "You ever watch one?"

Occasionally there appeared a tall mirrored office building picking up all the signs and lights and duplicating them endlessly. I was ashamed to feel something not entirely negative— though only a *little* something—gratified perhaps that my hometown lacked for nothing of the crap the whole country wallowed in. I suppressed one of those make-'em-feel-good statements with which I used to puff up my cousins on previous visits, so that they would forgive me for living in New York. I have given up graciousness—ho, ho, ho.

"To think this was all scrub when you and I went up north to look for jobs," Tom-tom said. (He didn't know I went because it was my destiny, and there was no use explaining.) "You could buy it all for nothing, but nothing is what you and I had. You remember old Santori whose grandson Tony married my niece

Shana? You know where his broken-down dairy was?"

He slowed down the car to almost a halt to get the full force of my reaction, and a car honked at us.

Impervious to other motorists, he turned his face as close to mine as possible without kissing and said, "You know where his skinny old cows used to range? And his children wished he'd let them move into town and work in the cigar factories? You know? One guess, come on."

"Come on," I said.

"The Tampa Stadium!"

I was not sufficiently impressed.

"Don't you follow the papers? It's the home of the Tampa Bay Buccaneers! Man, do you know what that place is worth? Just give me the parking lot proceeds, that's all."

He turned into some parking slots off the street. "And to top it off, the crazy old man, yes Santori himself, was still alive when that combine bought it for the park and he kept the house and two acres around it. He wouldn't sell them for anything. And he made the most money from that. It's now part of the Tampa Bay Shopping Mall, the big one! They made him an offer he couldn't refuse—ha, ha!"

The parking slot we parked in faced a small row of unlit small stores, closed for the day, except for one with a bright yellow window. Porn. I didn't have to look at it twice or read the no-minors sign to know. There was a girl in the dark doorway of the cleaners. Tom-tom gave her a hard look and she started towards us with a smile, but, thank God, she stopped when he quickly glanced away.

"You ever been in one of these peekaboo places?" he said.

"No, I'm still a virgin," I said. "What are we doing here?"

"I made a mistake," he said, improvising, "next block," and turned back into Dale Mabry again without look in his rearview mirror and let the oncoming cars honk without looking at them either.

"I don't believe you," he said about my never having been in a porno shop. "That's like saying you never been to McDonald's."

He made me laugh.

"I got news for you, Tom-tom," I said. "Most men have never entered a porno shop. For one thing, they're too embarrassed."

"You mean, you haven't gone?" he asked. "Don't it tickle your curiosity?"

He turned into the McDonald's parking lot and stopped at a slot closest to the street. He would not get out, obviously, until I answered him.

"OK, I been to one," I said. "On business."

"You write them books!"

"To get a big pink dildo with scales on it," I said. "There was someone I wanted to fuck, I forget who."

He loved that.

"Oh Pinpin, you gotten to be a dirty old man, I'm so glad." He got out of the car, locked it while giving me a look signifying that that was what Tampa was like now, and then with feigned casualness glanced around at the other cars. "You used to be so high-class—I mean, with books and all that—that I was worried you weren't getting yours."

He looked up and down the street too. He caught me watching him and he pulled his eyes away. I was on the point of asking him who that Dulcie was who had been seen on Dale Mabry, but I let it go.

"You want to hear something really shocking?" I said. "You're really taking me to my first McDonald's."

(Actually, it turned out I did the paying.)

He did not believe me, of course, and again threw an arm over my shoulders as we went inside. I looked at the brightly lit pictures of food overhead, the list of arch names they gave them, the young kids at the counter and beyond, at what I sup-

pose was the kitchen—stainless steel tables and stainless steel
grills, greaseless, immaculate. They weren't going to let a single
tasty germ come near the food.

A freckled girl took our order and placed a bunch of little
packages on a tray—oh, it was as much a ritual as doing the
stations of the cross—and then with bright eyes told me the
price. Hers was a perfect redhead coloring, my fleshly ideal. I
removed each bill from my wallet slowly, macho-like, and
handed them to her with a sudden look into her blue eyes. That
always held them and made them gulp or something. But no
more. She gave me my change and some vacuous greeting, all
in one beat, and was ready for the next customer before the
image of me had quit her retina.

I might have cursed my lot but for the memory of Cora drily
saying, her wide, thin lips, bloodless since she hit forty, opening and closing like a bird's, "Your delayed mid-life crisis, big
boy." Cora prepared me well for oblivion.

She had startled me then.

"What do you mean, delayed?" I said.

"You stayed in the swim too long, dear," she replied. (Unlike
me, she was always willing to reply.) "And you don't have experience in being overlooked."

It was already two years since the New York Times had last
asked me to review a book. "That's just what I'm a veteran of," I
said. "I don't even get mentioned when they talk about Hispanic writers."

"I'm not talking literature," Cora said.

We were in a motel restaurant, if you can call the dining
rooms in those places restaurants. The waitress had not laughed
at a sally of mine and I had said, Damn, they don't know what
service is any more. And that, of course, is what Cora meant.

I did not look at Cora, but I knew she was laughing noise-
lessly. That's the way they laugh in her family. Except when

they're really excited, and then they get shrill and horsey, as if they have managed to leap out of the stables. She had laughed that way when she caught me with Susie and it had become an unpleasant tic for me to live with. Twenty years now. She was nearing sixty; I had five years to go. She and Susie had remained friends; I lived in perpetual exile.

She continued, "They don't laugh at your jokes, they don't tremble when you stare at them. It usually happens ten years earlier, dear. I went through a whole evening with my slacks unzipped and nobody noticed. You've been very lucky. You've had ten years more than most men."

Sure, I could have been gallant and said something about her still inciting riots or some such nonsense that women like. I didn't. It was twenty years since she last believed a compliment from me. After the first flush, she would have given me that disconcerting cool look, and I had no wish to resuscitate my old Tampa Latin self. No after-you-Alfonse for me.

Anyway, she was flat-assed—how long did she expect men to look her way?

The fact was, Cora didn't mean to hurt or make me sad or glad. She did not care. It was a habit with her to say hurting things straight out; maybe only to get them out of the way. Flush them out of her system. Whereas Susie, being Jewish, would have said the same or much worse (she went for the jugular on the first leap) but would never have made me feel she did not care, much as she might have tried that as a ploy. Yet it was true that Susie also didn't care, but she simply would not let go. She cared for herself first; me as an appendage. I was her property. In either case, there was no comfort, no love. Or is that too subtle?

Tom-tom grabbed the tray while I was paying, and I let him go wherever he wanted. I was not about to hurry to eat that junk.

"I love to eat the french fries while they're real hot," he said, but I noticed that he went to a table at the front window, which was almost a long enough walk to cool them off but which provided a good view of the street. He was on the lookout, no question about that.

He flung fries into his mouth as he squirmed into his seat and with them visible as he spoke announced, "Only thing I don't like about McDonald's is they don't make chairs big enough for me."

I don't want to keep anyone in suspense about this: I didn't like the food.

God, I hate intellectuals who find one item, maybe even two, they aver are fine in every schlock emporium. Actually, a very good buy, my dear, et cetera. Like that writer for *The New Yorker* (I hadn't heard from them either in twelve years) who thought McDonald's breakfast was the best eggs benedict for the price anywhere. One thing I learned from Cora's idiot family: you want good clothes? you go to Brooks. You don't, in that case (but I figured this out on my own) have to worry whether what you select is in good taste. Food, however, they know nothing about, and there is probably a thriving McDonald's on Beacon Hill.

Still, I ate whatever Tom-tom left me. It did not start my stomach working or, for that matter, my juices flowing. It sat in my belly in a lonesome pile. Unlike Olivia's meal, my body did not reject it like an ape's organ.

And while I ate, I thought. It's not too bad, this return to Tampa. A night like this might happen at worst once a month. Or twice at the beginning. Fifty percent of my cousins would not, on their own, come to see me. The others would phone. Maybe. Invite me to eat with them Christmas Eve. Do they still do that?

Those great meals! Every piece of furniture in the house turned by juxtaposition into one long eating surface with table-cloths uneasily marrying their varying heights. At one end, with only oilcloth for cover and with the most battered utensils for use, us kids. Marvelous food and lots of it, and in the center of the table, almonds, hazelnuts, chocolates, and *turrones*, the ground almond sweets Spaniards eat at Christmas. And at our end the terrible din of happy children.

Strike that. It sounds like a television commercial of Thanksgiving in Iowa: prose always betrays me the first round; you got to rewrite, rewrite, rewrite. Clean out the shit.

Food soothes. Tom-tom hardly looked towards the street after all, but paused when he got up to buy a second order of french fries. (He paid for that one himself.) But Dale Mabry was not the kind of street on which people stroll or walk. Cities have no streets any more. They have strips like this one, and you drive up to where you're going like cowboys in the old westerns. Tom-tom must have known that sitting and watching the sidewalk could not have been the way anyone saw Dulcie or any other soul in Tampa.

Who was Dulcie?

The hell with that. I preferred to dwell on my Western simile. The idea that driving up to shopping strips or malls was not a corruption of mores that threatened to make Americans legless but rather a return to genuine frontier ways—that was more interesting.

No, it was not. Dulcie was.

I said to Tom-tom, "Are you expecting Dulcie to walk by?" It was like taking my finger out of a dike.

From the first rush of his response I gathered that Dulcie was his granddaughter.

Nubile?

No. She was young, but she was married.

I felt a lessening of interest that made me suspect, not for the first time, that I was as kinky as the next guy.

Then it occurred to me: "You mean, Junior really has kids?"

"Why not?" he said.

I had hurt him. "Sure, of course, I haven't kept up, you know," I said, and told myself that would be my last apology of the evening.

Junior had sired a boy and a girl during one of his first marriages. The girl was Dulcie, the boy a naval officer based in Rota in the south of Spain. I think I was told this too by my mother or my sister Celia, whose duty it was, they believed, to remind me of my Tampa family as often as chance occurred. You know, ethnic roots. Whereas I preferred to keep human contact down to editors and publishers—venial, true, but useful.

It made me seasick to attempt comparing Junior and his children with editors and publishers, in this McDonald's in Tampa, nowheresville in the land of the intellect. Maybe I felt dizzy because I had mistreated my stomach. First airplane food, then Olivia's, now this.

"Junior is happy now, though," Tom-tom said with assurance. "She's a very good girl, this girl."

He never answered my question about Dulcie, why he was looking for her now, etc., and I nodded to hurry him on, so we could go home. Home? The old house?

"They work for a condominium in Lauderdale," Tom-tom said, feeling encouraged rather than hurried by my nod. "I told you, it's a perfect situation. She works in the office, he in the out of doors. They give them a little apartment on the premises and all those old couples there love them. New York Jews, the finest people in the world."

He must have seen me calculate that Junior must now be near fifty.

He said, "I can die in peace. Junior is middle-aged and settled. I tell Olivia that. We don't have to worry what's gonna become of him anymore. You're a father, you know what that is."

Nevertheless, he leaned his head on one meaty hand and looked like a sad little boy.

"Hey, Tom-tom, Junior has a son and daughter," I said. "They'll look after him too."

Tom-tom looked at me as if I were some greenhorn who had

not learned the first thing about life. I thought of Crispin and Jared. He was right: I had learned things but they didn't stick. I knew you couldn't count on today's children all right, but I still went on saying reassuring things like a fool.

That's what's wrong with my books, those upbeat endings, those characters with hearts of gold, poverty in the forefront, rainbows on the horizon.

"Pinpin, I gotta tell you, I'm ashamed," he said. "Don't tell any of this to my sisters or cousins." He looked at me and so intently that he forgot to watch the street. "Junior's son Cheo—what am I saying! Chuck—Cheo is too Latin, he thinks. He's an officer in the navy. They promoted him from the ranks, they sent him to their schools. They promoted him all right—he won't have anything to do with Junior."

"He won't?" I said.

"Not even a Christmas card in six years," Tom-tom said. "Think of that."

I wasn't going to. Anyone who wants to be a navy officer I don't waste time on.

"I wrote him myself two years ago," Tom-tom said. "Actually, I signed Olivia's name. A grandmother, you know, has more, you know, pull."

"And?"

He reached across the tiny plastic table and held my arm in a tourniquet grip. "He's probably more ashamed of us than of Junior," Tom-tom said. "You know why—his wife once let it slip to Nancy Lee."

"Who's that?" I said, still believing in a tidy story.

Tom-tom made a face and said, "Nancy Lee is Junior's fourth wife," and added when he saw me calculating, "The one before this one." And he smiled for a second. "She said that Chuck is in intelligence and I guess that's why he doesn't want to be seen with Junior."

"Intelligence doesn't have anything to do with intelligence," I said. "It's spying, like peeking in at windows. It has to do with being a son of a bitch."

That made him feel better.

He said, "I mighta known you would say that. Just like my Papa Leandro, he wouldn't put up with high and mighty types. They gotta wipe their asses too, he used to say. Intelligence!"

"That Chuck sounds like a shit," I said. "But they're all shits."

"He was nice when he was a kid," Tom-tom said quickly. "Olivia and me had him for years when he was a boy, oh my. Dulcie too. You know, to give Junior a chance with his new marriage, so we took over the kids. And he was such a lively kid. He wanted to know about everything. I gotta admit he was intelligent. He called me Papa Tom-tom. So does Dulcie, but he thought it up. Listen to me go on."

I shook my head in self-rebuke: Tom-tom must be OK, doing all that for those children.

Tom-tom said, "We had the kids for two of his marriages, not one. The second and third. We raised them, I didn't mean to lie to you."

"I wasn't shaking my head about that," I said. "I was shaking my head about life. What about Dulcie?"

"What about her?" he said suspiciously. "*Life? Life* magazine? You used to work for it?"

I shrugged. "I'm just making talk. Let's go."

"Wait, wait," he said in his nervous salesman's manner. He grabbed my wrist, then said quietly, "Dulcie is more like Junior."

Retarded, I figured.

"Very sweet," he said. "Compliant."

I got up. How compliant, if they didn't know where she was? Isn't that what Lila meant by her being seen around?

"Wait, I'll get you another coffee," Tom-tom said.

I looked at the poor man. Leaning forward, with his arms

outspread on the table, he looked like a big toad. "What's the matter, Tom-tom?" I asked.

He brought one of his hamlike hands to his hilly bulbous face and rubbed it into a flat plain. "I haven't had a good man-to-man talk with a friend in years," he said, and he winked at me, as if we were having a dirty talk the way kids did at puberty. "You saw what it's like at home."

"Well, I'm going to be in town," I said, and added, to keep it vague, for I didn't yet know, "if I settle in."

"What do you mean?" He sat up, alert. "You staying?"

I said, "I mean, we'll talk again another time, OK? I'm tired. Must unpack. Stuff like that, my old cousin."

Imagine me, saying my old cousin. I must stop that slop. I'll end up like an old dog wagging my tail at everyone.

Anyway, it seemed to throw him off his track, and he got up mumbling, temporizing. "OK, OK, if you're staying, there's time."

He had accumulated a couple of extra trays during his trips to the counter and he began consolidating them.

"Yeah, yeah, this isn't a good place to talk either," he grumbled. "Maybe I'll get another french fries."

"Let's get out of here," I said, past impatience with his fumbling with the things on the table.

"To take with me," he said. "Not to eat here."

"Leave that alone," I said.

"Leave what alone?" he asked.

I started to walk away.

"Wait, wait," he called.

I bumped into a blond woman at the next table. There were two kids with her and they looked at me as if I were an old drunk. Actually, I was a little light-headed, but if they were going to stare at me, I wasn't going to apologize even if I turned over their table.

"Help me," Tom-tom said.

I went back to him.

"Here," he said, pushing one of the trays towards me. "You take this one."

"What're you talking about?" I said. "Whoever heard of—"

Tom-tom whispered, "We're supposed to clear it off." And he rolled his eyes to indicate that the other customers were looking at us.

"Me, clear the table?" I said. "I'm not a busboy."

I looked around. People looking at us turned back quickly to their food. They chewed seriously, looked vacant. There was one man at the far end of the room leaving with his tray in hand.

"See?" Tom-tom said. "You take them there and empty them in those tall bins."

"What're you talking about, you don't do that at home!" I said, my pulse beginning to race, denunciatory sentences forming in my mind, but only able to repeat, "What're you talking about?"

"You've got to hand it to them," Tom-tom said, oblivious of my indignation. "Each person tips his tray there and empties it and lays it on the stack and bing-bang, it's all done. Pretty neat."

I raised my voice without any effort. "Put back that stuff on the table! We're not working for them. Let *them* clear the tables."

"Pinpin, it's no trouble," Tom-tom urged, again in his softest voice.

It was the whispering that did it. The whole thing must be stopped. My ears tingled with the rush of blood. Still, I knew exactly what I was doing as I looked at him humbly fussing with the trays—no going mindlessly berserk for me—and I knew too what I meant to do and say; I was looking at myself doing and thinking and it all took on a crazy inevitability. I could watch myself but I could not, after all, stop what I was going to do.

"Put it back," I demanded. I grabbed his tray. He held on for a second while checking to see if I was serious. He then let go and because I was pulling too hard, the tray flew out of my hand, hit the back of a chair across the room, and clattered to the floor noisily.

"Goddamnit, you gonna work for nothing!" I said. "That's what you're doing, you know—working for nothing!"

"Hey, mister," one of the kids with the blond woman called out. "You dropped something."

His mother reached over and with one hand turned his head away from me and Tom-tom.

"Let him listen!" I hollered. "He'll learn something!"

Tom-tom scurried past me bent over to reach for the tray, but his paunch made it almost impossible for him to reach it and the cardboard litter around it. The tray slithered away from him; his fingers were too thick and he managed only to push it farther away, into a nearby table. A woman there lifted her legs off the floor, as if the place were flooding.

"I'm sorry, lady," he said. "I'm really, you hear." His breathing came heavily and his accent became totally redneck. "Ho-ho, I cain't get to it."

"Leave it there," I commanded again. "Do not touch it!"

A young man in one of their stupid red uniforms walked toward us from the counter, an arm held high as if greeting me from across the street.

"You want to do someone else's work!" I yelled at Tom-tom, then surveyed the tables, making sure they all heard me in this plastic palace. "Doing someone else out of a job, you are."

"Oh no, man," Tom-tom said, abashed and pleading. "It's nothing, just being polite."

"It's scabbing!" I said. I looked again at the faces chomping away at the fake food. "These bastards are making scabs of everyone who walks in here! You know that?"

The young man stopped a safe distance from me. "Sir?" he enquired tentatively.

Tom-tom was still stooping and I grabbed him by his belt and pulled. He dropped the tray he had finally managed to pick up. Two women got up from that table. One reached for her tray, the other picked up their bags.

"Leave it," I told them.

They kept their eyes on me and moved away backward, ready to change direction if I did.

"Can I be of help, sir?" the young man said. His voice quavered and he paled with embarrassment.

"Hire a busboy," I said. "Every one of you, leave your trays on the table, goddamnit!"

No question about it: they were all looking at me as if I were demented, not they. An insane bum, their faces said. Me, in a Brooks Brothers blue seersucker suit, a lightweight tattersall shirt, and a bright but sober summer tie, and they who had deliberately chosen to come to this parlor of embalmed food— *they* thought I was the crazy one.

Someone giggled.

I pointed in the direction of the sound. "Has it ever occurred to you to take those cardboard hamburgers back to the counter and say they are unsatisfactory? No, of course not. You do whatever they say. You have always done whatever they tell you."

It was a blond teenager in dungarees torn at the knee who had laughed. Pimples and a Louis XIV hairdo was all I saw. "Hey, old man, I like it—"

"Old man?" I said. "*You*'re old. If you knew what's what, you'd have a punk haircut and you'd respect your elders."

"Hey," he said, put out.

"But you'll be cleaning the place for them—you'll respect—"

The young manager spoke up. "Sir, I'll have to ask you not to . . ."

"Not to what?" I said.

"It's nothing, it's nothing," Tom-tom said to the room. "It's just a joke. OK?"

He prodded me with one of his hands, keeping a constant pressure on the small of my back, and I started towards the doors, but the young manager was in the way, paralyzed, terrified that I was heading for him with my wild look.

"Please," he said. "Let us make it up to you. Maybe you'd like a complimentary serving of french fries."

"See!" said Tom-tom encouragingly.

"Make up for what?" I said. I heard my voice crack on high C. "There's nothing in here I want. Nothing can be made up. You're all crazy—coming here, working here."

There was a wild laugh. I could not tell where it came from. Me?

Tom-tom threw an arm round my shoulders, trying to make it appear we were out for a jolly time, but he also exerted the same old push for the doors. A middle-aged couple coming in was mesmerized, unable to enter or retreat. The young manager backed toward the open space in front of the counters, where all activity had stopped, and the woman in the doorway finally pushed her husband to one side and screeched.

"He's got a gun!" she yelled. "Oh my God, don't shoot!"

The young manager ran behind the counter and disappeared with a crouch.

Tom-tom threw his arms out to the sides like an umpire making a decision. "Hey, lady, we're only fooling," he said. "There's no gun—come on, Pinpin, you've got everyone upset."

"Good!" I said.

The woman stopped screaming. "Oh, oh, oh," she said.

Then Tom-tom laughed his good-natured laugh. It was not genuine and no one joined in. "Folks, we're all friends," he said, but they still looked grim. The manager's head came up above the counter.

I threw off Tom-tom's embracing arm. I stood clear of everyone like a cowboy drawing his pistol in an unfriendly saloon.

"I'm getting out of here," I announced, good and loud, "and I leave you to your garbage and cleaning."

The woman in the doorway changed her mind about retreating and dragged her husband hurriedly inside. If I was leaving, she wanted in. They did not look at me as they went past, heads down.

"Thank you, sir," the young manager called out.

He made me laugh. Literally. I yippied like a cowboy riding a bucking bronco.

Tom-tom threw out his arms like a performer taking a bow, and taking them all in said, "See, it was a joke!"

"It's no joke," I said. "The joke is on you. You're staying, I'm leaving."

I knew they wanted to answer me but were too scared. What a marvelous feeling!

The automatic doors kept closing and opening with my comings and goings. I stood on the pad that kept them open, for one final taunt. Tom-tom had gone over to the counter, so I was alone like King Lear, more alone than he, for I had lost my fool. One final imprecation, something they could all carry to their graves. A malediction.

I yelled it as loud as I could—"Reagan voters!"—and walked as on wings to the car. *Maledizione!*

I might have flown over the parking slots to get to our car. I don't know how I got to it. I placed a hand on its roof to keep from levitating immediately. And to propel myself as soon as I was ready to soar. A fluttering in my chest began and I half-closed my eyes, the better to feel its delicate movements. It quivered like a bird caught in the hand. I must unclose it and let it go. I opened my mouth and felt its flapping climb to freedom. I sighed and saw in the brilliant square Tom-tom talking to the uniformed boy; he held a pointing forefinger to his own head and carried in his free hand a large order of french fries. I sighed again and the clambering bird escaped this time. Such release! Such happiness, happiness!

TWO

Why did I say there was no malice in Cora? Of course there must have been malice—aforethought, fresh off the griddle and warmed on a double boiler. Every woman hates her husband—after the first ten years. That I should exempt Cora is more evidence of the thrall I was in to New England Wasps. Not all Wasps, only the genuine Massachusetts Bay Colony Wasps; they're the ones, especially the Bostonians who with no effort can trace themselves to the Danas and Parkmans, all those characters, real in life or books—they're the ones who got to me, whose influence I must watch for and stamp out.

I first discovered them in the Tampa public library when I was a kid, and they have ruined my life. The Emersons and Alcotts and Prescotts. I used to roller-skate to the library from Ybor City—carrying the books in a bundle held together by an old belt of grandpa's—through the outer boundaries of where they (the dumb white Southerners) lived, putting on a sober and polite face when it was no longer Latins watching me go by, and I would come home, each Saturday noon, with another batch to make the coming week livable. A regular *Saturday Evening Post* cover, the sight of me. I knew it too: oh, what a good boy am I, I thought. No wonder I grew up into an intellectual.

There is a whole dark side to poor kids reading books with veneration. Mr. Carnegie should have been told about that while he was alive. Not just that he stole from the workers the money for those red-brick buildings. To start with, I believed throughout my youth that anything that was printed was, of course, beyond criticism. It was printed, wasn't it? That kind of attitude leads one—and this is what I meant to talk about—to judge everything, including women, in the dizzying light of dumb adoration, as I did Cora. You make a mistake about literature, you are bound to make a deadlier one about life.

Trouble is.

(I'm always saying, the trouble is.)

If presented today, as I was then, with a group of young girls eager to right injustice and change the world and willing to take me along with them, would I choose the one with Cora's background? Would I weigh one set of boobies against another, take a seismographic reading of each one's orgasms? Was it a matter of choice? Literary historians (mostly left-wing) go in for that kind of talk. Historical inevitability and all that. But I should know better: it was choice with me. The other girls (all members of Local 1250 of the Department Store Employees Union) didn't have a chance. They were all New York ethnics: Irish, Italians, Jews.

That doesn't mean they were all butting the gate of the corral stomping to get at me. But I was young and looked it. Once, after I had saddled her and we were lying around talking nonsense, I asked Cora what had attracted her. "What do ya see in me?"

Cora said, "Your brilliant smile. That row of perfect shining immaculate teeth. Your mind."

A few years later, when Cora was pregnant, I asked Susie too, also after copulation.

Susie said, "The way you move your ass."

I shook my head a little; I wasn't much for dirty talk between men and women, but I *had* asked.

Susie went on. "Also in front, the way your pants creased at the crotch."

Jesus.

She placed her hands on my buttocks and stroked them. "Beautiful," she said.

She embarrassed me.

She explained, "A nail's got to have a head if you want to drive it in."

I said, "You learned that at Smith?"

"While reading Faulkner," and she did something I won't go into.

Cora and Susie had been classmates at Smith. That's how come someone like Cora met the daughter of a Jewish accountant. (He ended up an investment broker.) They became friends and remained so. I cannot understand it. Such durability. It's more than I can say for Cora and me, though even through the worst of it that flat-assed tall Wasp and me never separated for more than a few hours. Stayed under the same roof, that is. Maybe Cora lived a little through Susie?

Despite the literary historians, none of us was responding, in the choice of mates, to historical necessity. Except, perhaps, Cora. Those big-boned, well-fed, and well-aired (summer and winter) Bostonians, they can't help but look at each candidate's teeth when contemplating procreation. Not his melting eyes or tumescent cock. They think of the future as an investment. I passed the test. After all, I am of good Celtic peasant stock, and mother fed me an egg stirred in fresh orange juice every morning of my childhood and youth, Depression or no Depression. They cannot blame me that Crispin and Jared became screenwriters.

Screenwriters!

They were not emulating me when they chose that life. It wasn't my genes at work. I went to Boston as wide-eyed as William Dean Howells a century earlier, missing every other breath as I circled the Common. The very phrase "the Common" gave

me an intellectual hardon. Of course there was no one for me
to call on, like the great patriarchs of literature that he visited.
Nor could I have. Howells, after all, was a New England Wasp
himself whose family had strayed to Ohio. Me, I was Cora's
working-class boy at best, but she had not told me then that her
family was as good as Robert Lowell's, nor did she ever later
come out and say so. She let it seep in. That's class.

She did not nudge me—ho-ho!—when I asked where were
we going and she replied Louisburg Square.

She was a Communist, that was the reason. (Just as I also
reveled in the Saint-Gaudens monument because it celebrated
not just a Shaw but a black regiment. Oh, we weren't all bad,
we two.) Anyway, who could they have boasted of that counted
with me in the Thirties? J. P. Marquand? He wrote Mr. Moto
stories. Robert Lowell? He came a bit later and he was a better
publicist than poet. He was all clogged up, metaphorically, just
as Cora suffered from constipation (the real thing) all her life.
Two hours of every day she spent on the john. Bran, prunes,
Ex-Lax—nothing worked. No more than Catholicism, liquor,
and young girls did with Cal: the poetry remained viscous.

I know now that the ground floor of that Federal house was
lousy with Chippendale and Irish crystal and ancient Wedg-
wood and that sacrosanct set brought from China by some flinty
sea captain, but then all of it simply seemed rundown to me,
and I thought, no wonder Cora lives unadorned in her studio
on Ninth Street—they're broke.

The furniture in the bedrooms I saw (they put me up on the
third floor; the servants' quarters, I thought, until I learned the
room was Jasper's, one of Cora's two brothers, away at Groton)
looked like it needed to be replaced soon. It was all early American, but I didn't know.

Cora did tell me that. "This is what I like," she said, in an
early version of her didactic tone. "What those austere Shakers
made."

And I said to myself, her folks must have sold the good stuff.

God, the fights years later between Cora and Jasper, her surviving brother, for those Shaker rockers and dressers and dumb boxes!

So spare that room was. Its self-imposed simplicity reminded me of the room in Ybor City I shared as a boy with grandpa. A linoleum make-believe rug between our two beds, two brass beds (probably tin coated with brass, and only one thin bar of it as headboard) each under a window, an oak dresser in between. It was all we could afford. That was Ybor City. But here on Louisburg Square, after I had taken off my pants and sat on the edge of the bed I noticed that there was also a night table with a lamp, not simply a bare bulb in the ceiling; also, a desk by the door held another lamp, and to one side of it there was a bookcase. The light in the ceiling was a kind of chandelier; there were three bulbs in it, screwed above what seemed to me crystal candy dishes. My mother owned a little serving dish like those, a marriage gift, and she took it out at Christmas to serve *turrones*, cut in small squares, to anyone who dropped in. If it was family, she said apologetically, "You have to use it sometimes."

It wasn't lost on me that whereas my mother worried that her dopey crystal dish might leave her open to the charge that she was putting on airs, Cora's consigned such ware to the ceiling of a third-floor kid's room. Imagine. I sat on the edge of the bed feeling (as we called that mood then) class-conscious. It was not much more than plain feeling sorry for myself, a useless emotion: you can't do anything with it but write sob stories. Still, it was keenly enough felt for the idiot I then was, and my penis under the voluminous GI shorts shriveled in sympathetic response.

Cora put an end to that. She opened the door and stood there but a moment in her nightgown and I immediately came to attention. I had never seen her in a nightgown. Later, while I

fingered the soft flannel of her gown and compared it with my
other hand to the softer and smoother flesh of her belly, she
repeated that of course I must have seen her in a nightdress.
Her mother inundated her with them—"She believes they'll
keep me chaste"—and I couldn't deny I had slept in her studio
many times.

But I was stubborn and insisted I had not seen one. I reminded her that we always went from clothes to bare skin and
back again; there was no in-between.

Cora emitted a little gurgling laugh. (We were now at her
bedroom at the front end of the third floor, for I was afraid I
might stain the bedclothes in the room I had been assigned. I
didn't, of course, tell Cora that.) Those were the times when
Cora was sexy. She grabbed me by what she called my handle
and said, "All girls have nightgowns, so now I know you really
were—ha-ha!"

I shook my head.

"God, I'm so bourgeois," she concluded.

After a moment, she added, "But what about your sisters and
mother. Didn't you see them in a nightgown?"

My mother! Merely to think of her in such a context was
enough to shrivel my penis once more.

"Goodness, you're so sensitive," Cora said.

She coaxed me back. That was one area in which she was a
superb coaxer; in others she gave orders, more or less. Though
she had a way of palming my balls as if weighing them on a
scale that gauged how many spermatozoa they contained. In
Germany she would've been a Nazi. In charge, of course, of
designating honorary Aryans.

Pay me no never-mind, as the black prostitute in Ybor City
said after first laughing at my manner. Pay me no never-mind,
sonny, you just look all you want. I had finally ventured, as
every Latin boy eventually did, beyond Seventh Avenue and
crossed the railroad tracks, my eyes gaping at the glossy black

women on the porches and the sweaty hand in my pocket squeezing a half dollar. I went up the steps of the first that smiled at me encouragingly and gave her my half dollar, which I knew was twice what I should pay. Pay me no never-mind, she said inside, lying on her back, her dress pulled up, and she chuckled and chuckled and it made her stomach fat ripple.

You can disbelieve the details of my stories about Cora and this black woman, but the bare bones are true.

In any case, the simplest things were erotic in the old days. (Expect no lurid foreplay details from me.) Being with her on that unfamiliar third floor in Boston, Cora's placing a hand on my knee during *Lenin in October,* our hands coming together on a subway strap—little things like that, unexpected juxtapositions and variations, aroused me, and, I suppose, Cora too. Why, it's a wonder to me that the boys walking today with their punk-dressed girls in the Village don't need to wear steel-plated jockstraps. Maybe they do? Is that what they mean by heavy metal?

This "wonder" only goes on in my head, of course. You know that you've reached old age when you start looking at young girls again. You're really old when you look at the fellows at their sides. I needn't explain, do I, that the boys are now our surrogates? And that it is all just wondering.

Where was I?

I needed to urinate. I won't go into why I always need to do this after ejaculation. Well, I must: I maintained with absolutely no volition a piss hardon and it is both uncomfortable and insincere. (If I've gone this far, I might as well say that Susie, not Cora—never Cora!—would yell at me that I only went away from bed to wash her off my genitals. For Susie, everything had significance: she was a Leninist without trying.) So there I was, on the third-floor landing with a hardon, looking back over my shoulder at the top of the stairs at the front of the house (tardily worrying about her parents on the floor below) while heading

for the other end of the corridor to the one bathroom that all
three bedrooms on this floor shared. There was a dim night
light by the bathroom door and I could see my way.

"Hi!" Cora's brother Jared said (we named our younger son
after him) and I jumped in place.

I hadn't thought to look toward the door of the room I was
using, his brother Jasper's. Jared stood there and he took a step
forward and stared. I placed a hand over it. He was definitely
looking at my penis. Was he a fruit?

"You're not cut," he said in that same flat tone of Cora's, like
a veterinarian making a comment about a dog or cat. "I was
hoping you were in your room awake. I wanted to ask you a
couple of things."

I had shriveled by then. "What?" I said.

"I guess you're busy," he said. "I should have known."

A helluva conversation, what with the setting and all. But at
least he wasn't, as they say now, gay.

(Why do I take that tone? I might have been open to fooling
around—earlier or later, though not at that moment. It is all
fortuitous; I mean, a lucky—or unlucky—accident.)

He had already started for his own room when I said, "I have
to, you know, take a leak, I always do," and he was gone when I
came out of the bathroom.

Cora had fallen asleep, more or less, and was taking up all of
her single bed and so I picked up my boxer shorts and returned
to my room. I didn't get in with Cora and snuggle. I was not
one for that after sex then. (It was Susie who taught me the joys
of it.) I didn't mind that Cora did not even notice me leave her
room.

The light was on in Jared's. Poor kid. I put on the boxers and
I knocked quickly on his door and walked in. There was a
frightened look on his face. He had been masturbating, of
course, but he was glad to see me, nevertheless.

He wanted to know about girls. For some reason I can't remember now—health, I think—he hadn't been sent away to prep school like Jasper and had, consequently, not acquired the confidence that comes with long, ignorant bull sessions with his peers about sex. He figured that a Latin working-class male like me was born all-knowing about such matters. I did my best by him.

About female orgasm I must have lied, but there were things I could recount: what I learned from the black woman in the shack by the railroad tracks, the heavy petting with a girl in high school whose buttony nipples hardened automatically at my touch and whose bottom wiggled at the same time, though she never allowed my hands below her waist. The rest of my knowledge came from Havelock Ellis, a Navy training film on VD in which Tim Holt discovers a chancre on his penis, and from my sessions with his sister Cora, though I never mentioned her name, naturally. Nor did he.

One thing I knew I should tell him: it's OK to masturbate.

He sat there with his eyes popping and both hands in his lap, covering up whatever there was to hide.

"Listen, Jared," I said. "Meanwhile, you're sixteen—"

"Practically seventeen," he said.

"Remember, it's all right to masturbate. It's no sin. I mean, beat your meat, Jared, your hair won't fall out."

He wanted to laugh, but his throat was too tight.

I heard myself quoting Dumpty, a loathsome, fat seaman on my gun crew. "Get yourself a large jar of Vaseline and make your hand as slippery as a cunt in heat."

I don't know why I said that. Dumpty and his soul-destroying view of sex. It shamed me the moment I got it out, so I said something worse.

I stood, and in a hearty locker-room manner patted him on the shoulder and said, "Don't worry, Jared, the day you get a girl naked you'll know just what to do. Instinctively."

The biggest lie of all—like most folk sayings and salt-of-the-earth knowledge. Someone probably picked it up from literature and infected everybody; it cuts across class lines, which is enough to make it suspect. But it made Jared feel good. As we used to say, go figure it out.

In fact, I put him so at ease that when I got up to leave he shook hands. Very funny, the two of us in our shorts shaking hands.

"Gosh, it'll be good having you for a brother-in-law," he said. "I know Dad's been making calls all evening—he's on a couple of committees in Washington and he knows the right persons to call."

Brother-in-law? "Uh-huh," I said and let myself yawn widely. God, I was sleepy.

"You know, when dad acts so serious as he did at supper—"

I was a polite fellow then and I hurried to say, "I guess he wasn't expecting some strange sailor for supper."

"For supper!" Jared said. "For son-in-law. Cora waited until yesterday morning to tell him."

"Hey!" I woke immediately. "Your sister told him we're gonna get married?"

"Sure," Jared said.

I had no idea; marrying Cora had been more of a daydream than a possibility with me. I had better find out from Cora, but I asked him anyway. "What did he have to say?"

"There wasn't much he could say, was there?" he said with a wise air. "Dad went to his study and then called mom and she didn't know either, so he called Cora back in and after she came out he stayed in there until supper. And after supper he went back in there, you noticed—that was to wait for answers."

Jesus Christ. Marriage! We were free spirits—or Cora was, working in Local 1250 on a volunteer basis and all.

"What's all this phoning about?" I asked, with some irritation: the old man shoulda called me. "What did your father want?"

"He wanted your serial number."

"My serial number?" I automatically looked at it on my dog tag. "Even I don't know my serial number."

"You don't?" He also looked at my dog tag, awed. "Cora does."

"What the hell is this all about?" I said, but I was much more timid then than that sounds.

Jared now spoke very cautiously, trying to figure out my strange attitude. "Well, if you're going to get married right away . . ." He looked at me again tentatively and then tried to regain that stiff Wasp composure. "You're planning to marry her, aren't you?"

"Sure," I said, and you could say that's when I proposed to Cora—while talking to her sex-starved, horny kid brother on the third floor of the house on Louisburg Square. "Sure," I repeated. "Why not?"

(Why not? Indeed. I could tell you now.)

"Isn't this something!" the dumb kid said.

"See ya," I said and went straight to Cora's room.

She was fast asleep, snoring slightly, content as hell.

I decided to wait until morning to ask her about all this. Even then, in the first flush of our love—well, second, in any case—I was a little scared of her. But, I said to myself, no later than first thing in the morning, she's got to tell me, before I have to listen to the old man say grace once more. (At supper he took me by surprise: I had picked up my fork before he began that we-thank-Thee business.) I didn't want him taking me off to the study and calling me to account without my knowing just what Cora had told him. Wasn't I supposed to ask for her hand?

I stood at the foot of her bed and hoped she would wake on her own. I concentrated my gaze and willed her to wake. That's supposed to work. But not with Cora: she's a strong personality and all vibes bounce off her.

Outside, in the hall, I again bumped into Jared. This time he was wearing a bathrobe. (I noticed that because I had never worn one. My Uncle Felix owned one because he had spent a week in the hospital for an emergency appendectomy; it was lent out to others in the family who got into the same fix.) I thought: the kid's sixteen, they come fast at that age. Had I been Dumpty I would have fisted my right hand and embarrassed him.

Instead, I said, "You got the midnight watch tonight?"

He loved that.

"I'm going down to the kitchen to eat something," he said. "How about joining me?"

I looked at my rumpled navy shorts.

"Oh, Spooner's got to have a robe in his closet," he said and went and got it.

There is a certain grandeur that comes with wearing a robe; at least, the first time. A toga and you could command empires. Even if your nickname is Spooner.

In those days I did not know or recognize paisley (Spooner's robe) or even suspect its uniqueness and superiority, and al- though I was new to refrigerators—not until New York had I seen any but those old oak iceboxes with the block of ice in the upper compartment wrapped in newspapers—I knew enough to recognize that the various doors on the wall in their kitchen, with heavy iron clasps for opening and closing what must be cavernous compartments, signified something grand indeed. Later, years later, when I accompanied Cora and her mother, after the old man died, to their bank, the safety deposit boxes reminded me of the refrigerator doors that took up almost an entire wall of the basement kitchen in that Federal house. I laughed. The young bank clerk, already pop-eyed with the strain of carrying the heavy steel box, turned to me with a star- tled look.

"Need a hand?" I said, echoing my offer of help to Jared

(long since dead, poor kid), who oblivious of the magnificence of their larder lugged a big ham to the work table in the middle of the tiled floor like any young Italian apprentice in the whole-sale meat market area of Fourteenth Street.

The ham came first, a full quart of milk next, though I could see a half-filled one sitting in the same compartment with bottles of soda and juices and cream. Jared piled up a grocery store on the table. Peanut butter, corn flakes, half a dozen kinds of cheeses I had never seen, jars of jam, mustards of all colors. It was going to be a feast, and after a calculating look at me, he brought out a second quart of milk.

He then removed a long slim knife from a rack in the wall, and in his left hand held out a squarish, black club that turned out to be a whetstone. Again, the first I had seen.

"Hey," I said as he began sharpening the knife. I watched his careful, precise strokes of the whetstone against the long cutting edge of the knife: more style in that, probably, than in his masturbating. "That's nice, Jared."

He said, "Dad began teaching Spooner and me to carve when we reached the age of ten."

"Began?" I said before I could censor myself.

"It takes a while, like everything else. Every cut of meat requires a different technique, a different knife," he said. "And fowls are something else." He looked at me suddenly: he was ashamed that he might have been boasting. He smiled shyly. "You're kidding me again."

"Naw, naw, you're good," I said. "I thought *you* were kidding."

"Why?" he asked. "Don't you agree?"

"Forget it," I said. "Let's eat."

He was a master at that too. He constructed sandwiches so thick that we had to open our mouths as wide as they could go to bite into them. We chomped in unison and skoaled with tall glasses of milk. We were divvying up the pies when Jared asked

me what month Cora was due and I said I didn't know before I
realized what the question meant.

"What did the doctor say?" Jared asked.

"I don't know," I repeated. "I been on board ship."

I couldn't eat any more.

He had already cut pieces of lemon meringue and pecan pies.
"Come on," he said. "You got to help me with this."

So that's what had been different about tonight: Cora hadn't
first run off to the bathroom for a long session, she hadn't left
me as in New York to throb in bed alone, and come back full of
jelly and the diaphragm. What had she done the last time in
New York? I could not remember about that.

"Pretty exciting, huh?" Jared said.

Sure, sex and war.

We were back on the third floor and I still could not think
straight. I should, of course, have left him in the kitchen,
waked Cora, and asked for confirmation, details, whatever. Instead, I asked Jared, "She told you only, eh?"

"Me? I walked in on mom and dad when they were discuss-
ing it, but you know how parents are—they told me I should
not barge into a room like that, without knocking. I had to
point out it was the library, not their sitting room."

"Your folks too, huh?"

"They didn't tell me a thing," he said. "I had to go to Cora
and she said yes, funny like, but then you arrived. Gosh, I
thought it would all be different when you got to be sixteen,
that you'd be in on everything."

It's not different even when you get to be sixty-five. I did not
know that then, of course. You're never treated differently; you
got to figure out things for yourself.

(After I hung up the phone—when crossed wires permitted
me to listen in on my sons talking about me—I was not only
abashed—a mild word for the eerie, trapped feeling I experi-
enced—but I suspected, I don't know exactly why, that Susie

had broken in Crispin. I *suspected*—but did everyone else know?)

I drifted off from Jared unintentionally without another word and failed him like the rest. Still, I had cause; he had dealt me a blow. I sat on the edge of Spooner's bed and a little ping went off in me, a string plucked and then its resonance damped, as if by a guitarist's left hand. Damped by a new thought, by the amazement that suddenly took over. I fell back on the bed and marveled about the—the thing I had started off in Cora's belly. I got a vision of our bodies moving in and out, that delicious slippery friction, and saw our sinful activity for the first time as a consecrated production unit. Hurrah for Marx! We had been literally making a baby and I doubled over on my side to keep from laughing aloud at the aptness of that baby-talk phrase. My child!

We had done it! I took a turn around the room, arms out and silently cheering. We'd done it!

I dashed out the room to Cora's. I meant to hug her and kiss her all over, but I stopped myself in time. She was busy; she was doing the needful now: she required her fecund sleep and I watched her from the foot of the bed while she sprawled across the whole of it in that way she had of taking it all, a madonna to me. I never loved her more than at that moment. There she was, fulfilling her destiny: making a baby on Louisburg Square, her natural habitat, a salmon upstream.

Men are different; we're nomads. We can pitch our tents anywhere.

I kept shuttling back and forth between my room and hers. Every time I had an idea or a question I popped up and ran over, but was always stopped by the sight of her asleep, a Wasp Raphael. Once, I even got a hardon but was so ashamed of myself that I shrank without an effort.

It took me a long time to fall asleep and then it was full of crazy dreams. (I don't believe dreams are interesting or significant and so I never describe them to anyone or write about them in my novels. The hell with Freud and Greek plays.) I overslept. Cora stood by the head of the bed shaking my shoulder and looking as she always did, slim and flat, not bloated as in my dreams.

To my surprise I said something I had not planned: "Why didn't you tell me?" and I placed my hand on her belly. "Like a cuckold I'm the last to find out."

"I'll tell you after you wash and shave," she said. "Your head will be clear then." And in a new (married woman) tone: "Don't shower—there's no time. Breakfast is in fifteen minutes."

I obeyed.

When I returned from the bathroom she was brushing my dress blues. "I didn't want you to be nervous yesterday," she said, and handed me the pants first. "Daddy can be very pompous."

"Shouldn't we have gotten married first?" I said. "I wouldn't have been nervous then."

"You want to marry me?" she said.

"Of course," I said. "You crazy?"

"Good thing you said that." And she let fall the hand holding the brush with relief. "I told father that's what we wanted to do but that we wanted his permission first."

"We?"

"It's important," she said. "We're going to need more than my little annuity."

I had seen the word *annuity* in books but had never heard anyone use it.

"I'm going to work," I said. "I'm going to support my family."

"You're going to college," she said, "and then you're going to write."

"I've got to learn about life first," I said.

She placed a hand on my hip and I said, "Do we have time?" She frowned at that and said, "One of your thirteen buttons is undone."

I buttoned it and stood at attention for her inspection.

"Pinpin," she said in a softer voice. "Pinpin." (She had found out my family's name for me and thought it fit in perfectly with her family's dopey nicknames.) "Pinpin. You're sweet to say you'll support me."

"It's customary," I said in my best suave manner.

She explained: "Mother and father didn't earn all their money. They got it from Gramps and he . . ." She made a gesture to show the shekels had been dribbling down for a couple of centuries. It probably began with the slave trade, I thought. "So we should get what is ours."

"Yours."

"Ours," she insisted; those were the days of our—well, yes, love.

"Even if they're reactionaries," I said.

"Oh, they're all more bourgeois than reactionary," Cora said. She gave me a little push towards the door, but also to stop my demurrals. "Let's get there before father—it makes a good impression."

I placed a hand on her right breast.

She snuggled against me as we went down. "They're so sensitive these days," she said.

"Who?" I said.

She explained. In those days I could have used an elementary course in almost all subjects.

I took my hand away and we walked down to the breakfast room sedately. My throat became dry as hell as I thought of what I was in for. Still, when we came upon the old man on the ground floor landing heading for the back, where the breakfast room stuck out over the garden, I dropped Cora's hand and said, brave as I could, "Sir, I want to talk to you . . . if I may?"

His eyes went to Cora first—with all the glare of a harbor light.

She said forthrightly, "I've just told him, father," but she kept walking away from the two of us towards the breakfast room.

The old man had no recourse but to blush.

"Sir?" I said.

"Very well, yes, of course," he said and stepped up his pace. He looked at Cora's disappearing figure and seemed to panic. He raised a hand to beckon her, but she was gone. He then looked at me and our eyes locked in a stare of mutual fright and dismay. It gave him courage to say once more, "Yes, very well." He looked again at the door to the breakfast room. "Let us have breakfast first." His eyes lit up; he got his bearings; he said, "No good talking on an empty stomach." A chuckle escaped him, but he stopped himself.

"Yes, sir," I said as if he were a ship's officer.

We marched in step to the breakfast room, silently.

Jared, the old lady, and Cora were seated waiting for us.

"Good morning," the old man said, and all of them brightened and said yes, yes, yes.

I was seated at the old lady's right and she looked at me benignly. I guess she approved. She and I faced the sunshine in the back garden and felt good, like Hemingway characters. There was a brick walk meandering about the garden. There were glasses and cups and plates at each setting—we weren't just going to have *cafe con leche* and a piece of buttered Cuban bread—and a woman I first thought was a nurse came in with bowls of hot cereal and a pitcher of warm milk and an open sugar bowl with brown sugar and no one talked to her. My God, I thought, this is a Katharine Hepburn movie! I waited; I wasn't going to be the first to lift a spoon off the table, but the old man never said grace.

He was as nervous as I was, no doubt. There are little clearings in my memory of those days; one is of that half hour that morning. Every detail is still with me, but I don't know what the old man ate. Almost immediately he was standing behind his chair and giving Cora a significant look and then nodding to me. He was gone and I still could not get my ass off my chair.

Cora said, "Father awaits you in the library."

Her mother said, "Now, Cora."

"Has he changed his battle plan?" Cora asked.

Jared giggled.

"It's the way you put things," the old lady said.

I stood, swallowed, and when no one said anything, I asked, "Where is it?"

They looked at me—Cora too—in a distant, inquiring way that made me feel like a hick.

"I mean, the library," I said, and I blushed to think they might have thought I was asking about the toilet, a question that young men of my background did not ask in mixed company.

Cora thought of it too and she gave a laugh that was a long shriek. A mean one. Something of a whinny. I should have known then and there she was going to turn that manner on me some day.

He was seated at his desk.

"I wanted to speak to you first, sir," I said, looking at the oil portrait of the old gent above the mantelpiece.

The phone rang and he grabbed it eagerly.

What a relief!

He mumbled and looked at me and I looked away to appear casual. A real library!—the Riverside editions of all the Wasp writers I loved. While he talked I looked for Thomas Wentworth Higginson. My hero, more dashing than Errol Flynn. A good bourgeois. Maybe Cora's family were good bourgeois. That's what my Cuban grandfather thought of FDR. I squinted and leaned towards the glass-fronted bookcases. I saw my face peering back like the little monkeys in the Central Park Zoo, big-eyed and worried.

He placed the phone back in the cradle with a satisfied look.

"That was mighty good of Tommy," he said. "I didn't give him much lead time, but your weekend leave is extended. You've got a week."

"I've got a week?" I said.

"Special dispensation," he said, and looked down to ward off effusive thanks.

I wasn't thinking of thanks; I was flabbergasted.

"Of course, Tommy knows I was at Groton with the President—we let in a New Yorker now and then. Ha-ha."

"What about in your family?" I said, as jauntily as I could manage. It was a mistake, of course; I saw that as the words came out of my mouth, but I could not stop myself. I made it worse; I explained. "I mean, in your family. Letting me in."

He was appalled.

His face frozen, he replied, "I thought you are from somewhere in Florida."

He was to be wary of me always. I didn't know how to play the game. It was for him to be jolly, to josh, even to backslap—if he'd had a mite too much. I was to sir him to death.

I tried, "Sir, I love Cora and I am going to do my best to make her happy."

His look said, that's all very well and good but can you support her? He shook his head to himself. The old bastard.

"I talked to Tommy," he said after I squirmed for a minute or two. "He's the special assistant."

I lowered my head in veneration. We Latins are born ass-kissers.

"About officer training," he further explained.

"Me?"

"He said just last week there was a new directive about enlisted men applying. Was it communicated to your group?"

"Communicated?"

I was stalling for time. I didn't want to be an officer. I wasn't brought up that way. That Cuban grandfather would kill me.

Rise with your class, he commanded. Cora believed that too, I think.

"Posted on the bulletin board of your unit," he said, then chuckled. "No place for that on a cruiser, eh? Read at roll call, I expect."

There was a certain approval of me in all this questioning. I swallowed and realized my mouth was agape.

"You have only to apply," he said. "Speak to your commanding officer." He lowered his voice. "It will be given favorable attention at the Navy Department."

Agape again.

"Cora tells me you attended secondary school in Florida," he said. "Actually, that may be in your favor—there's a belief in some quarters that Southerners make better officers. I wouldn't mention your evening courses at City College in New York. Errr . . ."

And like a fool I nodded.

"In fact, I think I'll call Tommy back and ask him to start the ball rolling," he said, my nod having made him expansive. "We can give him all the information on the phone that the application requires."

I said bravely, "Sir, I have to talk to Cora about that."

"Talk to Cora?" he said. He looked away for a long benumbed moment, and stared at a set of Longfellow. "Women like to be told what's in store, not conferred with. Keeps them calmer."

I said, "Yes, sir."

"But Cora is strong-headed," he added and chuckled a little and then became silent again.

I was right and I was wrong—about remaining an enlisted man.

If you're not going to get real equality, then you might as well let the other fellow do the worrying. The minor worrying. The petty details are out of your hands: you can lie back and let it all roll over you. No strain. But Cora? She had told me about the 1837 convention, the fight for the vote, Harriet Beecher Stowe's defense of Lady Byron, the provisions in the Soviet constitution, the muscles she or any woman can develop if she wants to pin the strongest man to the mat: I had to give her a say in our future.

I could not let her old man rush me into becoming an officer. I had already told Cora when I enlisted that I did not think a Communist should be an officer, even in a just war. A worker belongs in the ranks. Actually, I was thinking—an Ybor City Latin an officer in the United States armed forces? Fat chance. Yet here it was.

I would not be gold braid, I couldn't go around returning salutes, I couldn't enforce chickenshit regulations. Cora would be the first to agree. She had already resigned as educational director for the local and was getting a job in a war plant. Department store employees were practically middle class and certainly of no use to the war effort.

He allowed the silence to go on a little longer and then he smiled thinly, a kind of unsuccessfully hidden condescension for the young that adults indulge when their half-baked notions amuse them.

"No harm done if you and Cora talk it over," he said, a little gruffly for form's sake. "I can always call Tommy later or see him in Washington tomorrow."

He was, of course, a dollar-a-year civilian in government.

Let's face it, I was impressed.

He took out a gold cigarette case and offered me a cigarette. It was a plain Old Gold. I smoked Luckies, but I took it, to play the man-to-man game.

"It's been my experience," he said as he held out the desk lighter to me, "that women are more comfortable when men pile up tax-free bonds for them and on important occasions tell them what's expected of them. Even on not-so-important occasions."

I liked that. He sounded like a Shaw character. What's-his-name in *Major Barbara*.

He chuckled and so did I, like a fool.

Actually, what I believe now is they should be struck, in the Noel Coward manner. Like gongs. Who'd have thought I'd ever agree with that effete.

Encouraged, he added, "I am only repeating what my father told me when he gave me leave to charge the engagement ring to his account at Shreve's."

He chuckled again.

I shifted my admiration to his father. I should have known: it was those nineteenth-century bourgeois who were truly great. Audacious pirates, anyway.

An engagement ring! I had not thought of that.

"I shouldn't try to dictate the color of the drapes, however," he said and puffed on his cigarette and leaned back, giving me leave to do the same.

Again the fool, I chuckled along with him.

"That is one thing Pookey will not allow," he added.

Pookey? He saw the question in my eyes and explained, "My wife Felicia."

Pretty exotic. Those old Boston families can be daring with given names. On the next visit I met someone named Lasalle. A cousin, I think. They also let go their inhibitions with those Brooks loud summer trousers. And the lemon-yellow odd jackets. In summer, they stand around like tropical birds on their greenswards in Maine, getting pickled, occasionally making a loud noise like a macaw.

He put on a serious expression and without looking my way said that if it suited me that he could call Shreve's and have them open an account for me.

Agape again.

He waved away any possible thanks (that's not what was on my mind to say) and looked fearful that I might, God forbid, act effusively grateful.

"Matter of good business, of course," he said quickly. "They'd expect Cora to sign up with them for one of their china patterns, and should you ever think of living in Boston it's good to have established credit with the merchants here."

I came to and nodded, of course. I wasn't going to let on that I had no idea what he was talking about. I leaned forward and carefully flicked the ash of my cigarette into a dull metal dish he used as an ashtray.

"I see you like the Paul Revere," he said.

How long could I look knowing?

He pointed to the ashtray. "One of a pair from Pookey's family. It's passed on through the female line, so Cora will get it and I shall have to give it up to you. Bit of a matriarchy—ha-ha!"

And Cora entered, rescuing me.

"God, I forgot to knock," she said.

"New York manners," he said and I was glad I was not Jewish.

"Well?" Cora said.

"Tommy has arranged a week's leave," the old man said.

"That's all?" Cora said.

"There's a war on," he said.

"Father, I know that only too well. I warned you about fascism," Cora replied and took his cigarette case and extracted an Old Gold. "I mean, college and officer training."

I looked at her, but she was not looking at me.

I caught only the end of her old man's gesture—a hand held out in my direction and eyebrows lifted.

"Pinpin, didn't Dad explain?" she said in a voice so soft that it struck the tone she hit only during foreplay.

"College?" I said in a bewildered strain. "You think I should go to college now?"

"For officer training—you can contribute more as an officer," she said, meaning politically. "You see, don't you, how much greater your influence will be." And this time it was her old man's turn to be at sea. "Besides, it means two years of college at government expense."

"But you know I don't want to be an officer," I said, forgetting about the old man's presence and about politeness and all that, reminding her of our common ideology. "My place is with the enlisted men."

"Think of Robert Shaw!" She straightened, her voice took on its trade-union toughness. "What? What would you say of him?" She looked around for an ashtray with impatience. She picked up the Paul Revere and studiedly dropped her burned-out match into it.

"Really, Pinpin," she concluded. "Really, that's excessive rank-and-fileism on your part!"

No question about it, she was serious.

I needed to think it over.

There was a fire in the fireplace. I had seen Cary Grant—or was it the elderly Lewis Stone?—sophisticatedly reach out and empty an ashtray in just such a cozy fireplace. I would do the same. It would give me time to think of something to say.

Was I a hypocrite? Didn't I want to be an officer and wear cream-colored pants?

"Careful," the old man said. "It's pewter."

What's pewter? I thought, and the plate slipped out of my hand into the red embers of the log fire. Just as when Cary Grant was elegantly inept, I laughed.

The old man gasped, there was a funny whooshing noise in the fireplace, and Cora screamed.

You know what happens to pewter in a good fire? Look it up in an encyclopedia. It disappears. Pfft! Like Topper.

As one, Cora and her father looked at me—the outlander who had crossed the Rubicon of Beacon Hill—but no chemical reaction took place. I did not disintegrate. I did not disappear from their sight or their lives and I did go to college.

*   *   *

I never heard Cora scream like that again and we have had some terrible quarrels. I kept expecting her to sound that same thin high note many a time, especially on that back porch in Maine when she came upon me diddling Susie, but she was to keep her cool always. Of course, I never broke a plate from the old china service or dented the Queen Anne silver teapot or kicked the Adam sewing table, so I can't say I ever really tested her again.

Ha-ha-ha.

I am stuck with my ideology and my politics. One and the same thing. And they have failed me as much as Cora and Susie have. From that first visit to Boston on, I replaced my Tampa public library view of the New England Wasp with that of Marx and Veblen. But did that give me intellectual serenity?—no, no, no!

Serenity. Plenitude. Acceptance. I guess I am a hippy at heart. So why do I hate eastern philosophers? You tell me. The very word *guru* makes me want to throw up. I remember my mother saying to Uncle Pancho, "Oh, you don't mean the Gandy Bridge to St. Petersburg, you mean that skinny little Indian with the bedsheet!" and that is what I think of them all: pitiful little desiccated fellows trailing more of a sheet than they need to cover their puny, itsy-bitsy cocks and balls.

I had a load of serenity for a while. And plenitude. Cora, the boys (we immediately slipped and had a second boy, named after Jared who was, somewhat ignominiously, killed in training before the war was ended), and college, and seduced by the lacteal environment of our life, the easy acquisition of Susie as a robust—heigh-ho Silver, away!—sexual partner. She taught me a thing or two that Cora not only did not know but could not imagine.

A tiny bit of guilt. And some busyness with the kids occasionally. But such plenitude!

Cora came into another annuity. From a grandmother, I think; I never looked into her income closely and God knows she and her family never talked about money—unlike mine, who kept you up on how much they were jingling in their pockets every hour on the hour. Cora hired a housekeeper and returned to the union until, with the help of the FBI, the social democrats threw out the Communist leadership. (I don't have to explain my terms, do I? Social democrats are bums, politically and otherwise.) I quit the New School for Social Research as soon as I published a short story in *Story* and another in *New Masses* and was invited to lunch by an editor at a publishing house. He didn't get to publish my novel, because he lost his job when a social democrat (big in academia) wrote a letter to the big boss at the publishing house (the usual business dolt) about the editor's fellow-traveling politics.

What a time it was.

That novel—the one the editor encouraged me to continue—was eventually published in England where it earned me no more than its hundred and fifty dollar advance. Here it was widely read in publishing circles in manuscript and I collected a small pile of rejection letters that I can still bitterly recite by heart. I got six free lunches out of the manuscript, including the one with the editor who got fired. It was a story of noble ethnics from Ybor City, its hero a writer-warrior who ends up fighting on the Normandy beachhead—gloriously, of course. Just a private, a rank-and-filer, but invaluable to his captain, who tries to win him over to his General Patton fascistic point of view. But our ethnic hero is loyal to his working-class origins, and in the boat crossing the Channel for the invasion he and the captain carry on the grand debate, instead of shitting in their pants as any real soldiers would have done. It took me a long time to decide whether to kill my hero on the soil of *la belle France*, mother of revolutions, or to bring him back home to organize workers more glamorous than department-store sales clerks. I let him survive

and the captain die: I thought that would be an upbeat ending.
Ho-ho.

One thing the novel did for me with the Party—yes, *the*
Party—was to qualify me for membership in the cultural division. That gave me an opportunity to try for the job of movie
reviewer (I used to say film critic) on the *Daily Worker*. I got the
job because I was a noble ethnic, not because I had seen every
Hollywood movie released since I was ten, nor because I had
read Eisenstein and Pudovkin and could use the word plastic
long before it became a noun. So every Tuesday night, like all
Party members in New York, I met with my cultural branch
colleagues in someone's apartment, where we moaned about
the ghastly prose style of Party publications and were a little
disappointed if outside there weren't a car parked across the
street with two operatives checking attendance.

I believe those FBI agents went out bowling on occasional
Tuesdays and fabricated the roll call for the evening. Everyone
fucks off, why not they?

Where was I?

Oh yes, how women and politics failed me. Not like that
bullshit phrase, the God that failed. That's social democratic
hogwash. I mean failed in the sense that they were disloyal to
me.

God, it is great to speak straight out, bing-bang, and not
worry about plots and stratagems to keep the reader turning the
pages.

No more fiction, no more New Journalism. I'm an ex-writer,
I said. What freedom!

Though when I distance myself sufficiently and look at my
life, like a poseur at a museum, there was a plot at work in my
writing days that I did not create, and flat-assed Cora was not
above stratagems.

I am wandering again.

I was a writer whose wife had an annuity. A highly independent income. We lived in the Village, in cramped quarters at first but in the magic sphere of her college dreams—no farther east than Broadway, no farther west than Seventh Avenue, and of course uptown ended at Fourteenth Street and downtown at Washington Square: an area with not quite as much acreage as the family estate in Maine. It was her turf: if she saw a face twice that had not been around Eighth Street before, she announced that someone new had moved into the neighborhood. A good thing she did not work for the FBI, they would really have been efficient and no one could have got a passport and gone to England to write and direct movies there.

I could walk to work—25 East 12th Street was the Party building (it's condominiums now)—and also to Susie's on Jones Street. For fun I used to, sometimes, duck around corners and wait in a doorway hoping to see some neatly dressed agent hurrying by. No luck. I figured they must have had a camera going across the street on Twelfth Street, but Susie was a Party functionary and her place should have rated some surveillance too.

Susie's parents were progressive Jews, no matter how much money her old man was making on the market. They supported her so that she would be free to fight the good fight, a hangover expression from the Thirties. Whereas between my family and Boston there might as well have been a Maginot line, passports, visas, and border guards. Cora did not allow them to come see us in New York and we went to Boston only at Christmas. I don't know why Cora kept us apart as much as she did. There was not the slightest chance that we would fight: Wasps never talk about anything serious and they don't kiss and hug grandchildren and interfere in their upbringing. Not the ones from Boston.

Maybe she was a chauvinist, maybe she thought I was too volatile. But, in fact, I was always polite in her folks' presence. Bostonians turn me into the good little Latin boy from Tampa I once was; in their company I quick polish my scuffed shoes on the back of my pants' legs and stand at attention.

Otherwise, the McCarthy days did not scare me out of a single opinion. I did look over my shoulder often, and when I emerged from Jones Street I figured someone took notice, but as I said I never saw an agent. Susie was section organizer for the cultural division, so if you wanted to know which painters, writers, actors in the Village were Reds, you had only to keep an eye on her place.

Her apartment was on the second floor, and when the ground-floor storefront beneath it emptied, she rented it and began selling the kind of dresses and doo-dads that she first bought for herself in Mexico and Central America. She had enormous energy; the place thrived; it must have confused the FBI. Her store was colorful and full of light and there wasn't a petition in sight. Her folks stopped giving her money—she didn't need it—and they were so proud of her they donated her old allowance to good causes in her name.

"How do you do it?" I asked her. "How'd you learn?"

"Price everything astronomically high," she said without having to think it over, "and the middle class thinks it's chic."

Cora added, "And when you're having a fifty percent off sale, you're still making a hefty profit. Right?"

"Right," Susie said.

They were good friends. I had to be careful when I ran in heat to Jones Street or I might find Cora there with the boys. I would sometimes watch them talking together (Susie's unwavering respect for Cora's ideas, Cora's delight in Susie's shenanigans) and wonder how it would be to have them in bed together. Actually, it occurred to me only once: it appalled me so much that I am sure I paled.

Susie and I never once discussed my breaking with Cora and marrying her. It never came up. It was as unthinkable as breaking with the Party. I didn't have to skirt the subject. Susie was happy as she was.

Susie was a bachelor. She knew how to entertain a man (expect no details from me), and I believed she was faithful to me because she was not going to have any male around messing her apartment. At her place there was only the special smell of her person. It permeated everything she owned. I once picked up a sweater that she had forgotten at our apartment, got a whiff of her perfume, and immediately became hard. I told Cora I was going out for cigarettes and ran over to Jones Street.

And I always walked away from her apartment uplifted, pleasured, unthreatened. It delighted me that she was a bachelor.

What a perfect arrangement!

But I did not think of it as an arrangement. God, no. I thought—if one can say I thought rather than that I opened myself to the emotion—that this plenitude, this variousness of experience was a writer's privilege, his duty almost. In a stratum of feelings that fed such a notion there burbled the feral conceit that some men were not meant for monogamy. We were destined for chieftainship by our spiritual and physical dimensions.

No details, no details!

Everywhere you turned you bumped your nose into Freud. I picked and chose. Instinctual gratification was OK, but I skipped over the passages that debunked the old leering idea that male genitalia of a certain size was prized by women. I liked to throw in a good word for Otto Rank, who thought neurosis was probably a strength, not a weakness. The Party was very opposed to Freud, but in the cultural section we were all waiting for that to blow over like a thunderstorm.

Meanwhile, I only joked about how the old saws—big cocks mean good sex, et cetera—were still the best laws. I knew about love, that it soars above the physical; I wrote about it in my stories. I guess I loved both those dames. Who knows? But Susie was more fun.

I walked away from Jones Street taking big strides, feeling big-chested, manly. I give Susie credit for the way I treated the FBI agent who finally accosted me after one of our sessions. At last I was being taken seriously. He came up to me on Sixth Avenue at the corner of Eighth Street, just past Bickford's Cafeteria.

(That's the Bickford's where the Bohemian poets, like Maxwell Bodenheim, hung out in the worst days. They went in and bought nothing. There were catsup bottles on every table and stacks of clean glasses by the cold-water faucet, and that made a kind of Reagan meal. Now there's a Dalton bookstore on the spot, a three-floor affair with pretensions. Writers autograph their new books; Dalton's would even stock Maxwell Bodenheim if someone brought him back into print. Or even me.)

I do not know whether it is old age or that any place I pass has too many memories for me: I cannot tell a straight story anymore.

The FBI agent called out my name.

I smiled automatically, I was feeling good.

He reached into his inside pocket and brought out, cupped in his hand, the badge ensconced in leather everyone recognizes now more quickly than a condom. "I'm from the Federal Bureau of Investigation—" and the badge disappeared into his jacket—"and I'd like to ask you some questions."

"You're kidding," I said.

He pointed to the curb. Their car was there, his buddy in it—probably the one who was going to play the bad guy.

He said, "You're going to a movie? We'll drive you there."

I said, "And you want to ask me some questions?"

I don't know what—other than the glow of Susie—inspired me. I stepped back. I raised an arm.

He looked alarmed.

I yelled, "Everybody! Hey, everybody, listen!" I called to the people walking by or waiting for the bus or just hanging out. I waved both arms. "This guy says he's from the FBI and he wants to ask me some questions. Come on over."

On Sixth and Eighth you can draw a crowd in a second if your appeal is outlandish enough.

The poor schmuck began making grimaces and shaking his head as soon as I began yelling, and by the time I paused he was back in his car. Four or five people were looking in the window and questioning the two. "FBI? Really!" One man with a ponytail—in those days, ponytails were rare—kept grinning and asking them, "Are you really a Fed? I got some questions to ask you, darlings. Are you game?"

They drove away fast from the curb.

"A Ford, they use a Ford," an old woman said. "It figures. Henry Ford was the first American fascist."

"Naw," said the man with the ponytail. "Teddy Roosevelt."

A guy my age tapped me on the shoulder. "Did he identify himself? Show you his badge? They gotta do that, you know."

"He did," I replied but kept my eyes on the car out on the middle of the avenue, straining for the light to change. "I got a look at it."

"Are you a Stalinist?" the man asked.

"Aw, come on," I said.

"No, no, you got a right to be whatever you want," he said, "but you know some of the practices of your hero in the Kremlin are ruining our credibility—I mean, for the rest of us Socialists."

I pointed to the car as it went uptown past Kaiser's, that great men's store, and said, "They don't make any distinctions."

"You're right," he said eagerly, "you're absolutely right."

I knew what he wanted: a good streetcorner gabfest, Village style.

"So long," I said, then added, "Thanks," and strode along to Twelfth Street feeling triumphant. It was one of the best moments in my life.

Which should give you an idea.

Don't you doubt it, the reason the Feds stopped me on the corner of Eighth and Sixth (how dumb can you be: that is the heart of enemy territory for the Center to the far Right) is that I had written and published the first unfavorable review of a Soviet movie ever carried by the *Daily Worker*.

The first and the last.

A Pudovkin movie, no less. I who worshiped him and Eisenstein and D. W. Griffiths, those masters of montage (another word gone out of style) and had gone to the preview three weeks earlier primed for film insights that would give me a chance for the first time (this was only my second month on the *DW*) to write a review that could allow me to act genuinely modest among my friends. Head slightly forward and bowed but able to look Jay Leyda and other film esthetes in the eye and in the future to withstand the terrible glare of Pauline Kael.

Instead, what did Pudovkin make but a Hollywood historical stinker, Soviet style, about a Russian admiral of the nineteenth century who led his barefoot but happy sailors (they would call out his name joyously while standing topside in perfect, dress-right ranks on lovely antique ships) against the perfidious French and English. The Crimean War, this? Do they teach it in schools these days?

A war so devoid of ideals that I believe the word imperialism was coined to describe it. Ugh.

Bathtub views of the rolling seas. Floor-angled shots of Louis Napoleon's court made the very chandeliers seem malevolent. A terribly boring movie. Who wanted to get upset about its misrepresentation of the Crimean War? You just wanted it to be over.

Proudhon and his generation would have burst a gasket.

The equivalent for us: we have survived to 2050, the U.S.A. has a socialist economy; some southwestern mushmouth is head of state; and to please him Warner Brothers gets its top director to make a movie on Vietnam with Henry Kissinger as its hero and napalm as a sort of liquid balm. All to boost internationalism.

I wrote (very cautiously): maybe it has appeal for the Russians, who only recently broke the neck of the Nazi Army and are now having their credit for this achievement taken away from them, but for us it's pointless.

"That bad?" said the feature editor who happened to see my review in galleys.

"Worse," I said.

He gave me a sympathetic look.

That was the last one I got from him for a couple of weeks.

He had to go see the movie himself after the review appeared. "Why didn't you just say it was boring," he said. "Why'd you have to get into the Crimean War and Nicholas the Rod and all that?"

(I had been thorough.)

"I think it'll be all right with the Ninth Floor if you write your Sunday think piece on it," he mused, "and praise it from another angle. And maybe lay out some second thoughts on it to take back some—I don't say all—of your original reservations."

"I didn't have any reservations," I said. "It was all-out bad."

He did not listen. "You know . . . you went back to see it because its power as a film persisted in your mind and so you went back et cetera and had these thoughts."

I said, "You said you were bored."

"To death," he said, "to complete the phrase."

That session with him went on for two and a half hours—until his wife called and said he had better pick up some hamburger meat on the way home.

My compromise: "I don't go back to see it, but I say that I was wrong—"

"I didn't mean you actually had to go see it!"

"Wrong to call it pointless. With the cold war on, it says to the world that the Soviets stand ready to fight all aggressors. However—"

"What however?" he said. "Leave it at that. It's my night with the kids, I gotta go."

No, I should have to reiterate what a crummy war the Cri-

mean War was, and add a thought I had been too kind to in-
clude in my review: that it had been a dumb conflict to select
for carrying this Soviet message, since the Russians had been
the aggressors or, in any case, the ones who had started the
hostilities with France and England.

"Oh, God!" he said; rather, yelled.

"That's the best I can do," I said.

"I'll call you at home tonight after the kids are in bed," he
said on the way out. "Think about my solution. A simple statement: I was wrong to think a Soviet director of Pudovkin's emi-
nence would, in this day and age, make a pointless film period
paragraph. Think about it—you don't have to see the lousy
show again."

The Ninth Floor did cave in on me.

Let me explain. The Party building on Twelfth Street housed
the *Daily Worker* on the eighth floor. Every floor was Red: on
the ground floor the Workers Bookstore, halfway up to the
eighth was *Jewish Life*, a magazine for which Susie sometimes
did volunteer editorial work. ("Taking the Yiddish lilt out of the
copy," she used to say.) On the ninth floor was the Central
Committee of the Party and all the ideological heavyweights. So
now you see what I mean about the Ninth Floor caving in, et
cetera. We lived in our own world, spoke our own jargon, and
were altogether the most American of phenomena. I realized
this when Jared, for a moment, flirted with the yippies in the
Sixties. Oh man.

Susie thought I was wrong. She thought I had been confused
by superficial aspects of the movie, show biz elements that
should be beneath a Marxist critic. In other words, I had not
been deep enough. She had not seen the movie, of course.

"But you know, darling," she concluded, opening my fly and
winking, "we intellectuals are not to be trusted. We're too easily
corrupted by—well, everything."

I am tempted to describe what she did next.

Cora had to look up my review. I suspect she had stopped reading me after my first think piece appeared. She found three or four sentences with what she said were wobbly syntaxes, mere unglued dangling phrases. We had a long which-that, should-would argument and I said I did not care what Fowler thought.

"But what about it politically?" I said.

"Oh, I'm sure you're right," Cora said. "I wouldn't see that movie for the world."

"Thanks," I said and felt better. "What should I do?"

"Of course, everyone's thumping away at the Soviet Union these days, which is why you should not," she replied quickly enough and then smiled in a prune-lipped way that only she and the actress Edna May Oliver could; she always smiled thus after a jab at my solar plexus. "Write an apology, say you were wrong."

"Wrong!"

"Essentially," she said. "If you hit the Soviet Union, then you're on their side. Simpleminded, but it's a fact. There's nothing you can do about it."

"That dumb movie is *not* the Soviet Union!" I yelled.

I have to be provoked twice before I yell.

"Well, have it your way, dear," she said, happy she had made me reach my limit.

My Party branch stood by me. They were all writers, all restive about socialist realism, the anti-Freud line, the deadly novels coming out of Russia. A couple of them said nothing, but the rest threatened to write a collective letter to the national education director, go as a delegation to the *DW*, et cetera.

My editor got nowhere on the phone that night but arranged to take me out to dinner the next evening with Sid Savage, a nice guy who wrote a humor column. The discussion and arguments and laughter went on so long that we bought some wine when we left the restaurant and went to Sid's big bachelor studio. It was all good-guy talk. Not a word about the movie itself.

We were agreed it was a stinker, and yet we ended up arguing until breakfast.

Did I remember, my editor asked, what the *DW* had been like? In the army he had told himself that if he survived the war—it was about 2 A.M., the hour for confidences—he would come back to the *DW* and talk them into a tabloid form with at least two pages devoted to culture and entertainment. Regular movie and theater reviews, a dance critic, a music critic, a humor column: a real American newspaper.

Sid Savage opened another bottle of chianti. "Listen, I wasn't going to tell you," he said, "but I ran into Jack Stachel and he brought up the subject. *He*, not me."

Jack Stachel was the member of the Central Committee in charge of education and although no one believed he was very intelligent or, indeed, very educated, he was, at the moment, on trial at Foley Square and therefore a hero.

"He said that V. J. was asked for a report on the whole feature section in view of the weak political orientation that your review revealed. And V. J. said to them that your kind of review was difficult to do battle against, because what motivated your esthetic views—did you know you had esthetic views?—what motivated you, shall we say, was an unconscious anti-Soviet stance. So-o-o . . ."

"Unconscious?" I said. For me it was also the hour when having conquered sleep, I was, I thought, particularly lucid. "Doesn't V. J. know that's a Freudian concept?"

They groaned. Nobody liked V. J. We were quiet a moment, Sid opened a window, shooed the smoke out of his studio, and said, "Life, oh life!"

"So what did you say to Stachel?" I said.

"I asked him how his pinochle game was coming along."

My editor said, "You gotta apologize. They'll wipe out the whole feature section—even Lester's sports column on the back page."

"Apologize for being unconscious?" I said. "How do you do that?"

"Easily," Sid said, drinking out of the bottle now. "You saw the light. People are always seeing the light. Where would the modern novel and the modern theater be without the light turning on in the third act?"

My editor repeated, as if he'd just had a new thought, "They'll wipe out the whole feature section, they'll bring up your whole branch on charges, they'll—"

"Why don't they just fire me?" I said. "That's an old American journalistic tradition."

"You're the only byline writer in the paper with a Spanish name," my editor said. He leaned from the waist down and whispered, "It does not look good to fire a member of the upcoming minority in New York."

Sid Savage said, "No one gets fired, you know that. They see the light. With the help of our comradely self-criticism."

Finally, I proposed that they give me space to write a considered analysis of the real nature of the Crimean War, its place in nineteenth-century European history, and its relation to the defeated revolutions of 1848. And, not inconsequentially, how Pudovkin's blurring of the real truth of this configuration of events forced him to make esthetic choices that were patently imposed on the material—no matter how good-natured the reasons—and impeded any natural story development, so that the viewer unable to make sense of the action became bored and disbelieving.

"It would give me the opportunity," I concluded, "to deal with the phenomenon of boredom in art. It's not an emotion that just drops out of the skies, you know. It's a personal self-defense against untruth."

Sid Savage said, "You must be kidding."

Before we broke up that morning, I wrote a terse little statement saying that I was wrong to say the movie was pointless,

and it was printed in a box on one of the feature pages. It did
not help the movie stay longer at the one theater that ran Soviet
movies; Party members believed my review, not the disclaimer.

At least once a week I tested Cora. I asked cunning, seem-
ingly unrelated questions and they proved she was not reading
my reviews. Susie did. I was not entirely unhappy.

By 1950 they could not afford me at the *DW*. Nor a lot of other
people. I was somewhat pleased that they did not take me off
the payroll until the second economy wave. Cora thought it a
serious enough moment in our lives to merit talking about
money and income and other such matters considered obscene
in Boston. She said I could stay on as movie reviewer (they were
perfectly willing for me to stay on at no salary); her income was
sufficient. I said there was one matter I firmly believed in—not
just for my sake but for literature's too—and that was that writers must be paid for their work. Otherwise—

Cora stopped me. She understood, she agreed. There were
tears in her eyes. The boys were at school—Grace Church's, of
course—and we got into bed as in the old days. Political and
economic ideals and sex go wonderfully well together.

Cora drew the shades before she took off her dress. I almost
stopped her, for Susie had got me into the delightful habit of
letting the sun shine in on our naked bodies. No details!

I wrote a short story about a married couple who fall in love
again, nothing serious, a bag of beans, money on my mind, and
sent it off to the *Saturday Evening Post* using Cora's surname.
They bought it. Lots of people who thought art-is-a-weapon
were impressed that I made it in a slick. I myself pointed out to
Susie—who was an exception—that F. Scott Fitzgerald, et
cetera.

I woke up one night with the thought that it was that Boston
surname that did it.

I wrote another one, another bag of beans, about old Mrs.

Allen who amidst litter lived near us in Maine. I cleaned her up, of course; made her a dear old eccentric instead of the ratty, black-toothed character she was, and signed my name to it. They bought it.

At Christmas, Cora's father cleared his throat significantly when we sat down to dinner. He complimented me.

The old lady looked at me with shining eyes. (Not for nothing was she named Felicia.) "So heartwarming," she said.

Cora whinnied.

I bought—with my own money and for myself alone!—the piece of blueberry land with the little shed on it. I turned it into a writing studio. I did a lot of mooning there. I also produced some more beanbags.

Then, as in the old movies, the McCarthy period petered out and the Cuban revolution occurred. And my heart soared. Montage shots of rambunctious left-wingers in San Francisco making a mess of the Un-American Activities Committee hearings, of Havana one mass of wonderful-looking Latins welcoming the bearded boys come down from the mountains of the Sierra Maestra.

In between, the urge on me, we went off to Spain one year to live cheaply and to write without a stop, et cetera, while the boys were at a prep school that cost a hell of a lot more. (I never exactly looked into the bills; it was all involved with annuities and trusts and whatnot.) By chance, in Asturias, looking up an uncle's hometown, we stayed one night in an Oviedo hotel at the same time as Mrs. Franco (a long-faced, horsey woman who looked like a Boston dame) and the murderers in her husband's cabinet. I wrote an article about that. The *New York Times* bought it. I was suddenly a journalist!

Montage again: editors calling, me taking off for Havana, for Buenos Aires, for Lima; me at teach-ins being hugged by Abby and Jerry, and at Columbia and Harvard by my sons. Seven books in ten years: four novels (including the one about noble

ethnics) and three New Journalism. Lunch at the Algonquin
with Mr. Shawn; at Sardi's with Harvey Shapiro; in Maine, an
invitation from Mary McCarthy turned down with impeccable
Boston snobbery by Cora.

Freeze frame: the Seventies, me on the back porch, my hand
you know where, and Susie leaning back against a corner post
ecstatically.

Background music: Cora whinnying.

THREE

Tom-tom looked at me when he left McDonald's as if he too were floating—so happy, so grateful; but he did not embrace me with his hamlike, lung-collapsing hands only because he held complimentary large-size packages of french fries in each.

Nothing ever blinded him, however, and he said, "Why, you doggone old man, you enjoyed that!"

I kept a hand on the gritty, dirty roof of his car—to propel myself should I want to levitate again. Everything had calmed in me: the fluttering gone, the soaring urge grounded. I was serene.

"You were pale a moment there inside," he said, "but look at you now—hey, hey!"

He continued chuckling to himself as he maneuvered his bulk behind the wheel without ever letting go of the two handfuls of french fries. I could smell them, but my stomach did not turn over. That was a grand step forward for me: I'd yet become a first-class American.

"You look ready for a night of it," he said. "Here, hold one of these for me. No, I'll eat it right here. Fast. I know you don't want me to drag it out. I know I got rotten taste."

"I'll hold them," I said. "I want to get home."

"Home?" he said.

"Celia's and Cuco's," I said, like a little boy who had been corrected. I was shaken by the night's experience: would my yes-you-can-go-home-again project, a brilliant solution in New York, work? Would it? For I had meant it less as going home again than as holing up and keeping the enemy at bay.

I added, "Home for tonight."

"I thought that we could make the rounds a bit, like when Uncle Felix took us kids out in the Model A and we went over to Bayshore, remember?"

"I don't believe you," I said.

"But I remember, for chrissakes," Tom-tom said, his mouth full of fries, "the good old days."

We were already heading west on Dale Mabry—more of chickenshit America going by—and I said, "Come on, head back for Ybor City, I want to call it a day."

"Olivia will worry if I'm not out with you," he said. "That's why she let me go out, because I'm with you."

"That doesn't make sense. Go on your whorehouse visits by yourself, tell her you were out with me," I said, feeling a bit edgy again. "I won't give you away."

"Pinpin. . . ?"

"What do you want? There's something specific you want from me. Out with it. Don't give me the Bayshore Drive answer. Not tonight."

"Jesus, you're a Communist, you're supposed to have compassion."

"Where'd you pick up that word?"

"TV," he said, and laughed.

We had stopped for the light at the corner of Kennedy Boulevard (old Grand Central of awesome memory) and he now turned left towards what had been the Hyde Park section in the days when we went rubbernecking in the Model A. The upper crust lived here then, descendants of Scotch-Irish carpetbaggers pretending to be old South.

"You're going the long way round," I said.

"There's no fooling you," he said. He drew the car from the center lane to the curb and brakes screeched and drivers cursed. He paid no attention to all that; he tolerated it as background noise. His big hands were on me again and his eyes were wide and pleading and teary like our basset hound Sam in his last smelly days. "It's Dulcie. Only you would understand."

"You said we could talk about her another time," I said, amazed I remembered.

"It's no time for talk," he said. "It's time for action."

"You've been watching old John Wayne movies," I said. "I know the fellow who wrote those lines."

"What?"

"I used to know him," I said, and confused him even more. "I don't know anybody any more, anybody any more, anybody any more."

"There they go!" he said. "There they go—the son of a bitch."

He was faking. He kept looking back at a side street, but his eyes were unfocused and he shaded them with one hand, forgetting it was night time and the side street was dark anyway.

"Dulcie?" I said, keeping the skepticism out of my voice.

"In the van," he said and pointed vaguely.

"You're lying," I said.

He slumped over the wheel. He looked at me as if I'd wounded him. Then he began on the second package of french fries, which he had held between his legs and must now be one greasy lump.

"Why are you holding me prisoner?" I asked. "And cut the bullshit when you answer."

He protested. "I've been honest all my life!"

I insisted.

"It's true about Dulcie," he said. "She's in Tampa."

"Where else should she be?" I said. "What's it got to do with me? Now, I mean."

"And I thought you knew—we're your family," he said, aggrieved but still munching. "We're not important enough for you to remember, that's what it is."

"Come on, Tom-tom." That's all I said.

"We're not old-time Americans from Boston," he continued. "Pilgrims, pioneers, high-toned."

I waited.

"Just because we didn't come over in a covered wagon," he said.

I sort of laughed.

"I cannot go to my brothers—never mind the sisters, this is for men," he said. "For one thing, I'm the oldest and it doesn't look right. They're not serious, anyway. They gonna make it gossip all over Tampa and it'll get to Estela and her Mafia husband that I don't even talk to—"

I said, "Are we going to park here all night?"

"The trouble with you is your cranium isn't big enough for your brains," he said. "It makes you impatient, like an itchy crotch."

"You want to visit Dulcie and you want me to come along?"

"But I told you she doesn't live here anymore," he said. "She lives in Galveston, which is where her mother went to live when she left Junior."

"I *am* beginning to feel a certain pressure on my brain," I said, but he didn't laugh.

"She married a Marielito in Texas," he said. "Dulcie, I mean." He raised both his mitts and struck me on the shoulder. "There it is, it's out. Can you imagine what grandpa woulda said. She married a counter-revolutionary!"

"What kind of Marielito?" I said.

"One of the bad ones," he said. "The worst."

"The kind that hung around the Parque Central in Old Havana, I bet," I said.

"The worst," he repeated.

"How'd you let it happen?" I said.

"Who had anything to do with it? Olivia got a letter from Dulcie's mother when it happened—she thought it was good news."

"Olivia?"

"She's not that dumb—she's my wife. Dulcie's mother, of course."

"Start the car," I said. "Drive it wherever you want to go. I can fall asleep right here as well as anyplace else. There's no reason why I have to understand anything. All the things I thought I understood I didn't understand anyway."

Quick, he turned on the ignition. "I knew I could count on you, I knew it."

I almost said he should have spared me his wife's cooking, but I thought I should leave well enough alone.

"I didn't mean that about the pioneers and Boston and all that. I always liked your wife. But I don't want you to fall asleep. You gotta be on the lookout. They're in a van. I don't know if I told you that."

I said nothing; I knew it would sort itself out.

"Do we go to the Gandy Bridge first or to Hyde Park?" he asked after he turned off Kennedy, as if he didn't know we were already in Hyde Park. He slowed down at the first intersection and looked to me. "Left or right?"

"Suit yourself," I said. "Who the hell knows what this is all about?"

I stuck my head out the window and looked up at the corner sign. Swann Avenue. With two *n*'s. Oh, the power of literature! I was back in high school, still a virgin, the only person in Tampa who had read Proust. Only the first and third volumes; that's all the dumb Tampa Library carried. Swann, Odette, those lush dresses she wore—how did he get past all the layers without tearing some? Maybe that's why love was sad. I had tried unhooking a girl's bra—surreptitiously and, of course, while it was still on her—and it was hell. Swann! How I loved love then. I have always thought of it since as something you had to be well-dressed for and great literature as necessarily vague and boring for long stretches. I have never told anyone this.

When I came to, Tom-tom had driven straight ahead.

He was prodding me on the shoulder with jabs of his thick, steely fingers, then pointing ahead with the same hand. "There's Bayshore right there. We'll take it all the way to Ballast Point first. It's a good place to park for the night."

I said nothing. Why had I blanked out? Proust? The second time since I arrived in Tampa. Two blank-outs, one levitation—not bad.

I shook my head in wonder and Tom-tom said, "Yes, Ballast Point. Remember when I took you there the time you were convalescing? You were a kid and they had peacocks."

I asked him if he knew why it was called Swann Avenue.

He slowed down and turned into Bayshore Drive. "Though it's much too early for him to close up shop. Still . . . what the hell, we'll go anyway, and then Gandy Bridge, right?"

"Swann," I said. "Why Swann?"

"No swans," he said. "Peacocks they had."

We were a sitcom. That was my life, a situation comedy; no depth whatsoever.

The rotten smell of the Bayshore at low tide. No madeleine but enough to relax me. I leaned back and enjoyed my thoughts. The grand old Bayshore Drive of my childhood. Our heads stuck out the windows of the Model A and shrieking, we also managed to wave our arms out too, to point at the mansions of the rich. That's my favorite, that's my favorite! A heartbreaking little ethnic scene—ho-ho! That's the kind of thing I should have written, the stuff of Mary Pickford movies, the heart-tugging hilarity of Norman Lear sitcoms. The hell with the Gertrude Stein sentence, it's the Neil Simon one-liner I should have mastered. Ho-ho!

The prodding fingers, the car stopping at another curb, Tom-tom growling. Not growling—sobbing.

Sobbing!

"Ya laughing, ya laughing!" he blubbered.

He banged at the wheel. He grabbed me and hiccuped and let me go. He flailed his arms and bumped them into the roof of the car and into the windshield.

"What's the matter with you?" I said. "Who's laughing at what?"

My left arm hurt up and down and all the way through to the bone.

"I'm a frail old man," I said.

He really was sobbing. What a mess.

"I told you about Dulcie and you laugh."

I said, "We're trying to find her and her husband. What's so terrible about that?"

He wiped his face with one hand to get the tears out of the way, and he grabbed my arm with the other. It was like a tourniquet this time.

"God," was all I could manage to utter. It hurt so much I could not shake him off; my arm was paralyzed.

"You don't care, that's why. I have been ashamed to tell you and I been working up to it all night and then you don't care. You are not a compassionate person."

He let go of my arm as a final gesture of despondency.

The return of my circulation allowed me to speak. "I'm here with you, aren't I? I should be at home—in Ybor City, that is."

"It's your home now?" he said, as if that's what he had been making a stir about. He looked ahead reflectively—or was it calculatingly?—and I saw the moonlight glisten on some stray mucus his hand had not reached.

Quiet.

"All right, I tell you once more," Tom-tom said. He hiccupped again.

"Steady," I said and I could have laughed: a real soap opera line that, all right, all right, all right. Might as well add, "Take it easy."

It worked. Without crying, he said, "Dulcie has been turned into a prostitute. He gets the customers and sits behind the wheel of the van while they do it in the back."

I was wrong: there were tears on his face again, but only a few this time and not those fat, flooding ones.

He turned to me full face. "You believe me?"

I nodded.

"Poor kid," we said in unison, and he was so grateful that he patted me on my numbed arm.

He started up the car and we headed towards Ballast Point, the nirvana of our childhood when we didn't know about such things. That's not true; I think we always knew about the prostitutes by the railroad tracks.

"How do you know?" I said.

"I told you," he said.

"I must have blanked out. I'm sorry."

I had not said I'm sorry in months.

"That kinda news everyone tells you, they don't keep you in suspense," Tom-tom said. "First, her mother wrote from Galveston. Not to me—she don't like me—but to Olivia."

"She wrote about the business in the van?" I said.

"Not exactly," he said. "She said they had left Galveston and she thought they were headed for Florida."

He sighed deeply.

"What was wrong about that?" I asked.

"She said she did not trust him, the first we hearda that."

"So how do you know?" I said. It had possibilities as a story.

"Dulcie don't know she's a prostitute," he said argumentatively. "She thinks it's a game. You understand?"

"I don't understand how you know all this," I said.

"OK, OK, she's retarded," he said. "Everybody gets a bang out of saying it to me. And then they make me say it."

He wasn't answering me and I did not think I could continue to be what he called compassionate much longer.

"You notice all the new condominiums?" he said.

"You're crazy," I said.

"You know what I've been going through for three weeks? Have a heart. My brothers and sisters and nephews and nieces coming around and hinting. Heard the latest?—now the whores are doing it out of vans, saves on motel rooms. The way they say vans, I know they're sending me a message. They don't come right out, oh no. And they say whores, not prostitutes. No compassion."

"Lila didn't sound like that—"

But he went on. "Do they take me aside and tell me about it alone and spare Olivia? You know how glad I was when I got it outa Marina you was here? A person I could talk to. Like Aunt Mama."

I said nothing. I nodded, hoping that would keep him going. It would be a new kind of story for me to write.

He swerved left into a road with parking slots at the end; beyond them a lighted wooden pier, a kind of stand facing it, Tampa Bay all around. There were a dozen cars or more there, no one in them; they were out screwing somewhere no doubt, and I felt like exclaiming, "This is Ballast Point!" but let it go with a shake of my head and kept my attention on Tom-tom to encourage his talking about Dulcie.

He did not look right. Maybe it was the light there. Maybe it was those new kind of glaring yellow bulbs that did it. He was a brown-yellow color, more than a few degrees beyond sallowness, and he was panting, a candidate for a heart attack.

"Dulcie is my grandchild, Pinpin," he said. "It breaks my heart all this. I gotta save her."

"What about Junior?" I asked.

He lowered his head.

"You haven't let him know?" I asked.

"Junior is a sweet boy, he wouldn't know what to do," he explained, and looked at me searchingly, to see if I bought that. "Besides, I want to give his marriage a chance. Don't rock the boat with this trouble—that's what Olivia says. Right?" He grimaced and confessed, "Junior is retarded, I guess you know that."

He looked around as though he couldn't face me, and looked at the other parked cars. One of them in the shadow of an oak appeared to be a van. He jumped out, groaning and whooshing, and was back before I could get out. "Ohio license," he said.

"What do you want to do?" I said.

"Check the pier," he said and looked towards it. "Oh, Pin-pin, I hate those Marielitos. I hate all those refugees giving us a bad name."

If I were to write the story, I would omit the Marielito element. I'm sick of politics. A lot of good it did me; it was my fatal flaw. A political novelist, they said about me. They just meant that I was left-wing (if you're right-wing, they say you write about the human condition), and I was typed and shunned when the bad weather came. And in our country it comes at least every ten years.

Tom-tom locked the car carefully.

I surveyed the scene. This was Ballast Point? All the mystery gone. The trolley line used to end just about where we stood and the kids debarked with delight. Right here in the parking slots the peacocks walked under a banyan tree and there had been little cages for the smaller birds, whose names I didn't know but whose stances seemed taken for my delectation.

This was where my father and mother met, at a picnic of the Spanish social club. Did they kiss behind a tree? Was he respectful?

Tom-tom threw an arm around my shoulders. "Brother," he said. "Brother of mine."

We must have looked a sight—a couple of old men on their

last legs, hanging on to one another as our only means of navigation.

Well, they were a sight, too. Where do the tackiest people in the world gather? At Florida fishing piers. Stringy, leathery, blank-eyed. You cannot convince me they fish to gather material for great seafood fiestas. They survive on white, presliced American bread and gray, slithery baloney, the kind of stuff the seagulls pass up or eat on the wing, protesting, awk, awk, awk!

That's the kind of crowd that was there, a couple of their kids asleep by the smelly bait buckets. They made me feel finicky, and the shame of that made me more irritable than their looks really warranted. Tom-tom walked the length of the pier and back, stopping to get into conversations about catfish and Social Security and about how bad and wonderful everything is. I think that's what he talked about. The small talk of us Americans is all chickenshit. I didn't listen, I didn't even stand by and make friendly faces, but leaned on the railing a few feet away and looked towards the horizon where the phosphate plant's smokestacks now ruined the bay. I wasn't on the lookout for soulful thoughts. I'm not a Romantic-poet type, not me. I look for the worm in the apple.

Cora didn't simply whinny and then run from the back porch in Maine, she also said, "I came to tell you I could bring lunch out here, but now you may want to go inside first and wash your hands."

She clapped a hand over her mouth; she did not mean to be witty—nor could be.

"No lunch for me," Susie said and stepped off the low porch, lightly skipping over the bright cotoneasters, lithe in her chino skirt and Topsiders. "This really is your scene, Cora. I'll leave you to it."

I wanted to yell with indignation—"Don't go!"—but it would have been unmanly. "What, what?" I said, though for years I rewrote my reply (when at odd moments the scene returned to plague me) in order to sound as cool as the two of them.

I also remember saying, "It's a mistake, it's mistake!"

"My surprising you?" Cora asked. "It didn't occur to me to knock, since I was not entering the house but leaving—" Again, she covered her mouth, but as quickly chuckled and looked equable.

"Cora, Cora," I said and stopped: I was about to say, I can explain this, but my writer's sense saved me from that inept cliché, if cliché is the right word.

A great Groucho Marx line, however, but I was witless at the moment. There was Susie's figure gaily disappearing up our long driveway and I was trying to extract some story from the tableau we had composed that I could offer to Cora as alibi and reassurance.

"Pinpin, Pinpin." She used my Tampa nickname, which meant that she was being forgiving or gentle or whatever; not waspish, in any case. "It's all right."

"Cora, I don't know what came over me, I swear," I said. "It means nothing to Susie—she's not you."

She looked down and away and I saw, beyond the dry skin and spreading freckles and gray hair, that shy sideways glance that years earlier only sexual longing brought out in her.

"Cora?" I said.

"It is all right, Pinpin," she said in the slightly crackling voice that went with the softness. "I've known."

"Known what?" I said, as if this had happened only once.

That would not work. I then said, "Cora, let me explain," but I could think of nothing.

She looked at me and waited. Only a moment, however; she was never one to stand in line or suffer inattentive clerks: it was my brightness and quickness she had liked. She gave me another second, and said, "Susie keeps me up on the whole affair."

I thought of saying, It's you I love, Cora, but I asked myself if I'd be believed and it was too long a hesitation.

Then she whinnied.

I saw Tom-tom miss me, thinking I had walked ahead of him on the way back and left the Ballast Point pier. He rushed forward with all his bulk in motion. It must have taken the propulsive energy of a missile at launching to get him going at that speed.

"Pinpin!" he called, and stopped and peered towards the parking slots while he caught his breath. Then he stumbled sideways and grabbed the pier's railing.

I was afraid he would have a heart attack. "Tom-tom!" I yelled and ran down the pier.

What a show we must have put on for that audience. Coming and going, we must have made a lasting impression on those catfish fishermen.

He grabbed my sore arm again. "I thought you went!"

"Where, for chrissakes?"

"I don't know."

"Well, I don't know either," I said.

I laughed. It didn't sound as bitter as lately.

He hugged me. He kept an arm on my shoulders as we walked to the car.

"I got worried," he said. "I'm counting on you. You my lucky star. Remember that song?"

I had to say it. "Tom-tom, what do you hope to do? I take it that they are in Tampa, but if you find them, what can you do that won't make it worse for Dulcie?"

"What's that?" he said. "What do you mean?"

"I'll stay with you no matter what you decide to do tonight," I said and looked him in the eye and risked having him crush me with a hug again. "So that's not why I'm asking, understand? But what will you do if we find them?"

"The same thing you would do," he said quickly. "Bring her home."

I leaned against the car and said, "But that's not legal. He is her husband."

"So what?"

"You have to bring charges against him first," I said. "Go to the police and take him to court."

He shook his head, he lifted his arms. "That's crazy," he said. "That means lawyers—expense!"

At that moment a van drove in and parked at the slot closest to the road. He was launched again and I had to run after him to stop him if necessary. A Minnesota license and, up front, two old folks who had once been blond. Tom-tom switched gears with amazing agility. "Howdy, folks," he said and walked back to meet me halfway, his southern friendly mushmouth smile still lingering on his face.

It was his acting ability that irritated me. I said, "Is that what you're going to do? That Marielito will simply knock you on your ass."

"He'll have two of us to deal with," he said. "I saw you run to help me, little brother." He pointed to his bloodshot eyes. "I observe too, you know."

I said, "He'll knock me on my ass with no trouble."

In the car it occurred to me: "How come if she's in Tampa, Dulcie hasn't come to see you and Olivia?"

"She doesn't know about such things," he mumbled. "Let's go to the Gandy Bridge."

"OK," I said and felt like a Keystone Cop chasing after him eagerly. Of course, she doesn't know how to get there on her own.

If I were writing this story, it would be bound to have an unhappy ending. How the hell do you squeeze hope out of such material? I was sick of what my scriptwriter sons called my down endings.

"Right," Tom-tom said, guessing some, not all, of my thoughts. "Dulcie probably doesn't know she is in Tampa. I will kill him when we find him."

Christ.

"Think about it," I finally said. "They may not be here at all. Lila's daughter only *thought* she saw Dulcie on Dale Mabry."

"You remember that?" he asked. "So you did care."

"That's what Olivia said to you," I said. "God knows why I remember. That's my problem."

Too many details, I said to myself. The old naturalistic tradition. I don't have to remember everything.

"They're here," he insisted.

"Well, then, why wouldn't they come to you?" I said. "It doesn't make sense."

"I knew you're too smart," he said. "*He* came to see me, the son of a bitch—there, now you know everything."

"What else haven't you told me?" I asked. "Out with it. What fool's errand are we on?"

"Don't get so suspicious, Pinpin," he objected. There was no room in the car to gesture, so he grimaced a great deal to make up for it and thus made me feel my vision was blurring. "I could not talk in front of Lila and Conrad Dupee."

"Dupee!" he repeated and laughed falsely. "Conrad, isn't he a scream!"

He didn't like my silence, so he added, "And I had to spare Olivia's feelings."

"Well, isn't it going to worry Olivia more that you aren't back from Ybor City yet?" I said.

"No woman tells me when to come and go," he said. "Anyway, she knows I was going to ask you to help me."

"She was in on this too?"

I had been had again. I sat there quietly and thought it over. So what if he had deceived me? I wasn't out of pocket or harmed—except for Olivia's meal and his tourniquet grip. My stomach made a protest at that, and I swallowed to keep whatever was coming up down.

Tom-tom watched me with a hand on the ignition key, and waited.

"Why'd you allow Dulcie to leave with him when he came to see you?" I asked, to trip him. "Not that I care."

"Dulcie wasn't with him, he came alone," he said with an air of great reasonableness. "Don't talk that way. Of course you care, you're a compassionate person—don't go against your own nature."

"Let's get out of here," I said.

As he drove onto Bayshore Boulevard again I took another stab at it. "What makes you think Dulcie will come with us? He's her husband."

"I'm not asking her, I'm taking her home."

"Just like that, huh?" I said.

"Of course," he replied. "You don't ask women, you tell them."

"You should at least first report them to the police—"

"You think the police care about one more girl doing what Dulcie's doing? You know what goes on at every street corner?"

I said, "I mean, in case there's any trouble later. You can point out that you had reported them, et cetera et cetera."

"What do you mean, trouble?" he said, a little too macho for my money.

"I mean, when he knocks you on your ass while I stand by and referee," I said.

"He's not gonna do anything," he said, untouched by my argument. "And you're my cousin and you care too much for me—"

"Guys like him are violent," I said. "He also knows that the police can't be bothered. You have to be prepared."

Tom-tom shrugged. "Look in the backseat."

There was a rifle there. God, why hadn't I seen it?

"Are you crazy?" I said.

"No," he said. "You said I should be prepared."

"When did it get there?" I said.

"When I went to get you at Aunt Mama's."

He had prepared all right. "You got a permit for that?" I said.

"He's done what he done to my little Dulcie, I need a permit?" His shoulders shook a moment and I didn't bother to check if he was crying. That was probably an act too.

"I'm getting out of this," I said.

"You said—"

"I said let me off. I'm not having anything to do with this insane ploy of yours," I said, and moved about in my seat as if I could really get out. "Let them work out their own problems."

He started poking me in the arm again. "You talk like it's some tea party. You think our grandpa woulda let us be kidnapped into slavery and do nothing about it?"

"I didn't say to do nothing. I said go to the authorities and take her away from him legally. Prostitution, white slavery, is against the law."

"The authorities! I can't even get them to take that Children Playing sign off, you think they will do anything about Dulcie?"

We must have been swerving around, for a car honked and Tom-tom stuck a hand out the window and gave it the high sign.

In order to use both hands to explain convincingly, he parked on Bayshore along the water's edge, where it is not permitted. "This is the only way to do it. Quietly. The police will know nothing and neither will my brothers and sisters and there will be no talk, talk, talk."

"You think you can get into some fight with a gun at the Gandy Bridge and steal Dulcie away—who may well resist and holler—and nobody will notice?"

He hit me on the arm again. "It will be very simple. I'll show that Marielito the business end of my gun and he will run like they all did at the Bay of Pigs. And you will escort Dulcie back to our car."

"Just like that?"

"Sure. If there's anyone around sticking their noses in or if by a miracle the police show up, you will explain it to them in your fine English and there will be no problems. You're a very respectable person, Pinpin, don't you know that?"

"Is that why you want me on this expedition?" I said, and insisted on an answer with a hard stare. Is that why I had lived the life I lived, to serve as decoy in a whore-rescuing raid?

What was so wrong about having two women? I was faithful to them both all my life. Except for the time I went out to Hollywood. And that was at the invitation of a mogul—to discuss the dramatization of my novel about the Hispanic businessman, not because I lusted for Hollywood or other flesh—and at his party in Beverly Hills I woke up to some starlet bringing me to life orally. It could have been a male starlet for all that I cooperated.

I threw a fit at Cora when she told me she had known all along. You could have heard me all over Penobscot Bay. Not that anyone ever said a word to me. (The natives, like natives anywhere, know everything, but they don't let on to people from away.) Cora's mother was dead, and her father stayed at the main house with a full-time nurse. Our boys were on a bicycle tour through France or making student movies in Prague or Rome or laboring glamorously with some archeological expedition. And Susie was not staying with us; she had finally married a very assimilated, non-Israel-minded Jew and they owned a house in another cove and belonged to the yacht club, not to sail but to test its social bias. The yacht club race was on for the next day and I didn't go then or ever again. I finally declared my independence of all those Boston and Philadelphia Wasps. But Cora and I stayed married and under the same roof or roofs.

I guess throwing a fit was a ploy as transparent as Tom-tom's.
It almost didn't qualify as a ploy—it was psychologically inevitable—but it was a ploy, nevertheless, and it took me several
months to recognize it as such. I was the injured one, the dupe,
the betrayed. (This view has a certain objective plausibility and
it comforted me.) Little by little, Cora let me know (actually, I
asked her obliquely) that Susie had told her not only about me
but about every male in the cultural division of the Party and
about the occasional husband who strayed into her shop alone
to buy his wife a gift. She even made goo-goo eyes at an FBI
agent who was waiting for a customer to leave before whipping
out his badge. And she recounted it all to Cora while it was
going on, a kind of "Masterpiece Theater" serial that cemented
their friendship.

Cora intimated (never said so outright, she was too loyal a
friend) that Susie faked all her orgasms.

Actually, these revelations brought Cora and me together
again. Or helped. Sexually, I mean. She was much looser in
bed the next time. We never separated. It was not laziness nor
lack of moral indignation on either side that kept us in the same
apartment. We came from cultures that had taught you to stick
it out. Louisburg Square and Ybor City had that in common.

But I never again, as I said, showed up at the yacht club, and
I spent most of my time in Maine in my little studio in the
middle of the blueberry barren.

And, slowly, I began to see Susie again when she and Cora
got together. They kept up their friendship, of course, a subject
about which I was unable to pry much loose from Cora: she
blabbed only about the past. One day, after I had come back
from South America, where I had met with guerrilla leaders,
Susie and I came face to face at a protest meeting where I had
just spoken and she just laughed and reached out a hand to my
nether regions.

"Sex and politics are a dangerous combination," I said, and
for once I did not get a hardon for her right away.

But what the hell, it was the late Sixties. (Her husband Ira was in Cuba hoping to pave the way for American tourism there—the revolution needed hard currency.) Better than sleeping with all those available college girls and hippies to whom I only represented my subject matter—revolutionary Cuba, guerrilla warfare, the Third World—and who wanted everything out in the open.

"They're luscious," Susie said, "but have you seen the statistics on VD?"

That was not my reason—I just was not a cocksmith—but I did start sleeping with Susie again on a regular basis. Women think we're satyrs, but it was my constancy, my faithfulness, even my belief in marriage that brought me, you could say, back to her.

Not to the Jones Street apartment. She and Ira, an entrepreneur like her, now lived on Fifth Avenue near the Met and the Stanhope. (Ira, like many old Party members, knew how to make money; he was in the art business too, and would not touch nonobjective art for esthetic-ideological reasons, but there is more money in American nineteenth-century landscapes than I had imagined.) Susie first opened a second shop on the upper West Side, then another on Lexington Avenue in the Sixties, and finally—"A dialectical leap!" she declared—in the Long Island and Jersey shopping malls. She was as big as he (gross sales) and as apt to be away on her own on business. Like me, they were both New Left. Susie's shops were Third World chic: the price of an African basket at one of her places would have kept an entire village in Mali well fed for a year. Ira talked endlessly about realism in art, but you would have had to be an idealist all right to pay his price for a Hudson River painting.

Only Cora remained in the Party. Right? Right. Boston Wasps can be wild but they are never flighty.

Ira thought the world of Cora. "You're right, you're right, darling," he would say and give her an enormous contribution to whatever.

Susie and I would meet at the Gramercy Park Hotel. Upstairs in the room. We never ate in the dining room, never walked in or out together. Susie promised that Cora would never know. I watched Cora closely after our first trysts (our pace was slower than in the past) and she did not know. At least, I think she did not know.

Note this, this is a fact: Susie served as a model for all the Hispanic girls in my stories.

Which gives you an idea how smart critics are.

I know East Coast Wasps and Jews and no one else.

Well, maybe not.

Little by little the magazine editors stopped calling, the pub-date party invitations evanesced (if there is such a verb), and the requests to speak or to be a judge on literary panels did too. I had never hustled; I had never called an editor first. How relieved they must have been that I had the good manners not to embarrass them when this right turn of Lenin's train flung me out into the brambles of the undesirables. I'm sure they wished it were not so.

Of course, one always has the option of talking bitterness in the *Nation*. You want to publish in the *Nation*? Go ahead, publish in the *Nation*.

A simple heart. That was my mother, all right. And my aunts and uncles. I don't know about my father; he was perhaps simply not talkative.

God knows I am. I should have saved myself for the typewriter more often.

A simple heart is what I am not. I am vain, egotistical, ambitious, envious, and cold.

I believed the *Times* reviewer who praised my authentic Hispanics. Believed it? Gloried in it, I recall with disgust.

Maybe I should tell now what I discovered worried Cora about me. She was already sick when she wrote it. It was an unfinished letter that I found in her desk when she went to the hospital for the first time.

"I worry about him and socialism. He should not be tested by it. He's so good now, so angry about all the injustices and snobberies that boys of his background suffered. Still suffer, that is. Which is why he's such a good radical now—he resents it all so. But under socialism, when we will have done away with class distinctions, there will be no place for his anger to go. Can he stand not getting even? Can he stand being just like everyone else?"

Just like Cora to be beside the point, still thinking about the future, as when we were young and speculating about socialism all the time. Like her still belonging to the Party. And to say so in a letter to Susie, whose psychological understanding was primitive, to say the least.

Cora had cancer and it went on and on. Thank God, she wanted no attention, and it was her doctor who told me, not she. I was in the midst of a novel and had to turn down the first assignment for the *Times* in years to go look at Pinochet's Chile and, by the bye, go over to Valparaiso and see what had become of its great brothels and waterfront cafes. My first reaction (I'll be truthful) was that Cora was interfering with my career. This was the only magazine to call me since Allende was overthrown. I had been reared, as I've said, in the Spanish manner and I had done nothing during the months and months it took for her to die, in and out of the hospital again and again, so that I came to feel relief when she did. I'll repeat that—I had never hustled.

In true Cora style, I said so after she died, perhaps too soon and too bluntly, and my sons turned cold and bitter with hatred. (What can you expect from screenwriters?—sentimentalists by trade.) So did Susie, but she only for a while. It wouldn't have been her style. She had just returned from China where for a month she was a guest of the government. They wanted to pick her brains about how to set up shopping malls and she was acting as if she were Krupskaya. "You gotcha revolutions mixed up," I told her. "The Chinese are a bunch of capitalist roaders, all right, all right, all right." That's how we quarreled about my so-called lack of feeling when Cora was being incinerated.

Anyway, Susie was no longer fucking me, or anyone else, very likely.

Notice that last modifying phrase. A simple heart I am not.

Tom-tom was surprised that I objected, as he put it, to my being called respectable. "You are an author, a respectable person," he insisted. "I bring you along, like insurance. What's wrong with that?"

"Don't worry," I said, "I said I'd come with you and I will stay with you until you give up."

His hand was on the ignition and he took it away in order to hug me with both arms. "You're really family, Pinpin, not like my brothers and sisters."

I got a whiff of McDonald's french fries. "OK, OK," I said, "but let's get home before dawn."

And at that moment a van passed us. He said, "A Texas license!"

"That van?" I said.

"There they go, oh my God!" he exclaimed.

He fumbled with the ignition, flooded the carburetor— "Calm down, calm down," I kept saying excitedly—but he managed to take off while the van was still in sight.

"You don't want to pass it," I advised. "You want to keep it ahead of you until it stops."

"That's right, right," he said. "Oh my God, oh my God, this is the moment of truth."

There was no trouble keeping the van in sight. There was no other car on the Bayshore. It was the old part of town. Today's Model A's out for the evening go only to Dale Mabry and the shopping malls.

"Thanks, Pinpin," Tom-tom said and he hunched over the wheel as if to see better. "I was going to ram it. With Dulcie inside too—I wasn't thinking."

"No, no, you just want to follow him," I said, "and stop when he stops and talk to him. No ramming, for God's sakes, and no guns, just talk, remember?"

"Just talk?" Tom-tom said.

"Shouldn't he have turned a long time ago?" I asked, "if he was going to the Gandy Bridge?"

"Yes and no, you can get to the Gandy Bridge many ways now," he said proudly, never too worried to pass up an opportunity for boosting Tampa. "How can I just talk to him with what he's doing to my Dulcie?"

"How do you know he's done anything to her?" I argued. "Did anyone see him and her and. . . ?"

"They said that somebody said that a friend had, you know—"

I nodded to show that I understood the friend had been a customer and that I was not so indelicate as to require him to spell it out.

"You think they could have been exaggerating the way we all exaggerate?" Tom-tom asked, hoping for a yes.

I did my duty: I nodded, and it was no wonder, as he did a double-take, that he hit the man on the bicycle.

He did not, in fact, hit the man or the bicycle. He came so close to both that the man abandoned the bicycle with an astonishingly agile leap and one bicycle handle attached itself to the door handle on my side. A freak outcome. The bike moved along with the mad elan with which as kids we rode the rear ends of trolleys.

Cursing, Tom-tom was forced to stop. He might otherwise have gone on (for the man was already on his feet looking fit, more or less) whether I objected or not. I, of course, had objected, and he slammed on the brakes hard and the bike left us and went ahead on its own, having detached itself from the door handle as if from an irksome date.

I ran after it. It finally lay down on its side at the curb, quietly, the least perturbed of us all. What am I doing? I said to myself when I caught up with it. Right out loud, I said it. There was no one to hear and I needed the release.

The van had disappeared. Half a block back, Tom-tom led the man to a brick bench. The man appeared to be struggling to shake off Tom-tom's helping hands and to be looking my way for his bike. I waved—why, I don't know.

The bike felt and looked intact and I called out, "It's OK," as I walked it back. It was one of those skinny affairs, the kind it requires no muscles to ride up the Alps. Thousands of gears they've got. I exaggerate, as Tom-tom might say, but you get the idea. The kind of bicycle New York swingers take into Central Park and get attacked for by muggers waiting in the bushes.

They were in conversation when I reached them. Rather, Tom-tom was talking and the man, a trim old man our age who had not, like us, deteriorated, looked interested only in his approaching bike. I already did not like him.

"He's my cousin," Tom-tom was saying. "A famous author. The most famous author Florida ever produced. You know anyone to compare with him?"

The man did not even bother to shake his head; he leaned over to look at and touch his bike as if reading braille.

"It seems intact," I said.

"He knows all about them," Tom-tom told him. "He has two or three up in New York. That's where he lives. Authors can't live in Tampa, they gotta be up there where the action is."

The man wore a jogging suit. He perspired but would not allow himself to pant. He smelled like a refined locker room, not like Tom-tom. There was no sag in his arms or face or neck. He placed one hand on the pedal and I recognized him. A high school athlete of my day. An American, as I would have described him then.

"You know who this is, Pinpin?" Tom-tom said; then quickly explained to the man, "I call him Pinpin, a family nickname.

Even if he is a famous author and lives on Park Avenue."

The man sat on the bike and tested it by bouncing a little on it. "Well, I guess there's no harm done," he said and then clammed up, ashamed to have talked to derelicts like us.

"Good," I said.

"Tim Shane, that's who he is," Tom-tom said, exceedingly glad that he was not going to be sued. "Remember the ice cream plant?"

I nodded and said, "You played quarterback with Hillsborough," and was immediately sorry: he had not said he knew I was a famous or nonfamous author.

But Shane became less distanced. "You went to Hillsborough High?" he said, on the verge of admitting me to the human race.

"I had to go somewhere," I said. "Like Gooden."

Tom-tom forced a chuckle to make my comment sound friendly.

"Yes, it's all niggers now," Tim Shane said.

I said, "And the mayor of Tampa is a Cuban nigger, but a Republican, of course."

Tom-tom tried to chuckle again, but it didn't work.

"Good pedaling to you," I said and left them for the car.

In a moment Tom-tom came back too, and got in on his side as becalmed as if he had brought off a coup and indiscreet high spirits might jinx it.

Tim Shane pedaled away with a last, mean look at us. As soon as he looked ahead only, I stuck my arm out and like Tom-tom gave him the high sign.

"Careful," Tom-tom said, then chuckled with no effort, his melodious low rumble. "Fuck him, the big shot."

"We'll never catch up with the van now," I said, hoping he would take me home. "You can't have any idea where they might have gone. If it was they."

I hoped he would say no. Instead, he said, "I have an idea," and frowned as he waited for Shane to get out of sight before starting up the car.

Shane switched to the sidewalk a block away, and a couple on foot had to flatten themselves against the parapet along the water's edge to accommodate him.

"It wasn't my fault," Tom-tom said, getting ready to start up the car. "He's a rotten biker."

"People still walk along the Bayshore," I said, talking as inconsequentially as any Tampa Latin.

"Oh my God," Tom-tom said, back to his anxious manner. "Duck, duck quick."

He reached over and grabbed my neck and pushed my head forward. It just missed the dashboard.

"Down, down," he insisted. "It's Felo."

"What? What?" I resisted; I was not going to ride with my head between my knees. "What fellow?"

"Felo, Felo, my brother," he said and threw up his arms in exasperation. "It's too late. Felo, your cousin. Look at the son of a bitch. If he wasn't always hanging around women I'd swear he was a fairy."

The male of the couple Shane had just passed hurried towards us. The light of the bay was behind him; he was only a dark outline to me, but apparently not to Tom-tom. I could not call up any image of Felo's face. He was slim, I could see, and his head was a fuzzy top and he moved in quick but not smooth-flowing lopes, as if his joints were not well greased, which at his age they should not have been.

"How old is he?" I asked like the fool I had turned into. "Strike that—I don't care."

"Say nothing to him," Tom-tom whispered quickly. "That beauty parlor of his is a newspaper gossip column—he'll talk forever, God. Maybe he won't recognize you. I won't tell him."

"I'm not incognito," I said.

"Look at that old piece of meat he's with," Tom-tom said disdainfully. "Why does he bother?"

And Felo came into the light of the street lamp and the fuzzy top turned out to be the kind of frizzy hairdo I last saw on Susie four or five years ago. (Now everyone is punk.) Felo's was a light brown color with gray highlights, and he wore—wore is the right word—a set smile on his face that you could call an all-purpose smile. He was even thinner in the light or maybe his pants were too tight. His many-colored sport shirt was open down to his belly button and, of course, he wore a gold chain.

"Aha," he said. "Aha."

His lady friend stayed at the parapet and turned her back to us. She had the dead, flattened ass of a woman way past fifty.

I stuck my head out the window to help him recognize me.

He stopped as if his balance were precarious. He raised a hand, palm out like an old-time traffic cop. "Pinpin," he said. "Something told me. I knew it was Tom-tom's old wreck—"

"What do you want? What do you want?" Tom-tom said. "Pinpin has just arrived. No one knows he's here, so don't start broadcasting it."

"Marina knows," Felo said. He held out both hands to capture one of mine in them. "What are you doing with this riffraff? Is he selling you real estate?"

Tom-tom said, "I used to make him masturbate me when we were kids and he has always held it against me."

"He is so perverted that he still tries to get me to do it," Felo said, in a slow precise manner, the smile coming and going but never entirely disappearing. "Gives you an idea what kind of a sex life he has."

"Who's that piece?" Tom-tom asked.

"Besides Marina, who else knows Pinpin is here? Was there a shindig at your house and you didn't call us?" Felo paused; he would not let his brother off the hook. "Guilty, huh? Olivia has fungus you-know-where and he, my big brother, is too stingy to pay for you-know-what for himself. Massage parlors were made for old men like him. Can't get it on their own. Tell me, Pinpin, how long have you been here? Don't let them keep you from me."

I made a clean breast of it.

"Lila and Conrad, huh? Conrad Dupee!" he said and chuckled, and Tom-tom laughed too. "How do you like that pair? I don't let Lila in my beauty salon, I lose business if she just sticks her head in. I saw her today and I came over to warn my brother but here you are."

I said hello a second time.

Keeping his face sideways to Tom-tom, Felo said warningly, "Lila wants one of your apartments."

"*My* apartments?" Tom-tom said.

"You can lie to me," Felo said, "but Lila is another matter. She's a sweet innocent thing and deserves better."

"We gotta go," Tom-tom said. "Pinpin has to get to bed. He's not a well person."

"Maybe I can take my friend home," Felo said, "and join you."

"None of that," Tom-tom said. "Go home to your wife."

"It's not what you think," Felo said. "What does he mean you're not well, Pinpin?"

"There's no time to talk now," Tom-tom said. "Get your hand off the car, we're leaving."

"Come in my car," Felo proposed to me. "It's a new Pontiac, four doors." It seemed to remind him to open the door of this one and he did. "She's a refined lady, my friend, I'll introduce you. I am helping her with a problem. She reads books, maybe yours too, Pinpin—I was about to ask her."

"Close the door, close the door," Tom-tom called.

"You don't want to go around in this old wreck, Pinpin," Felo said. "You're going to your sister Celia's, right?"

"She's dead and you don't even know it," Tom-tom said.

"You think he cares about anyone in his family, Pinpin?"

Felo continued in his same even precise manner. "Celia, who is in heaven as everyone knows, came to me every week for a wash and set. I took her myself. She was closer to me than my brothers and sisters, especially this mad old miser who has you prisoner in his broken-down tin can and won't rent an apartment to his own sister."

"It's all right, Felo," I said. "I'll see you in a day or so."

"You can stay with us," Felo said. "My wife will take care of you—she used to work in a nursery."

"Pinpin is not an infant!" Tom-tom said. "Close the door or I'm taking off and the hell with you."

"I mean, Pinpin, that she knows first aid," Felo said. "We have an extra room—it's all yours. The children are gone and even the grandchildren."

"Good-bye, he doesn't need a hand job," Tom-tom said. "Good-bye."

"I'll come by tomorrow morning after I open the salon," Felo added. "I'll let my assistants take all the appointments and we'll go to lunch at the top of the new hotel downtown, my treat. You can see all of Tampa from there—it is the marvel of the century, it spreads out on all sides and you will see how your hometown has grown. It's very desirable, you need a reservation."

"I'm warning you," Tom-tom said and revved up the engine.

Felo said, "We're all keeping a lookout for Dulcie."

"What! What!" Tom-tom said.

"Anything new happen?" Felo said and closed the door without looking Tom-tom's way.

Tom-tom placed a hand to his heart, and I felt sorry for him.

Felo winked at me and gave me a half-salute.

Tom-tom zoomed off, cursing.

Tom-tom's zooming was mostly noise: the car wasn't entirely a wreck but it was not speedy. Actually, we harrumphed away.

"He don't know anything, he's feeling me out," Tom-tom said. "Don't worry, we'll find them, I promise you that. I got an idea."

I said nothing.

"That was a sample of my brothers," he said. "You already saw a sample of my sisters. You see why I count on you to look for Dulcie? Walking on the Bayshore with his piece of meat! Every time I see him he's got one of those females who go to his store. Salon, he calls it! They're all old. The young ones only want a haircut."

I said, "What does Felo want from me? Why's he taking me to lunch and all that?"

"Watch out," Tom-tom said. "He's got a lot of money. He owns that beauty parlor and the two houses on each side and it's right off the corner of Kennedy Boulevard. You know what that's worth? Watch out."

"It's a bore," I said.

"What's that?" Tom-tom said and then headed off any reply. "Maybe he wants to give you a hand job. Ha-ha! How I love to kid him. It gets to him. I tell him, you got those soft hands now from the beauty parlor, you oughta be very, very good."

"Tom-tom, you talk dirty the way we kids did in Ybor City," I said, disgusted with his never answering my questions.

"I know what bore means, you know," Tom-tom said. "That's not nice—we're family. So what if Felo . . ." He threw up a hand and waved it indeterminedly. "Am I a bore too?"

I had thought of something he might not want me to think of: "How come you're so sure that was his van?"

"Here, we'll turn here," he said, temporizing, God knows why. "It's old Hyde Park, but the termites have taken over."

"How did you recognize his van?" I insisted. "You only met the fellow, you didn't go around in his van."

He turned and slowed down with great concentration, a hand up asking not to be distracted. It was one of the grand old side streets, gone badly to seed all right, all right, all right.

"How'd you know it was his van?" I said once more. "You said it was a Texas license, but I couldn't tell and you're as blind as me."

"It was his van, I tell you," Tom-tom said. "I saw it before."

"You did?" I said. "When was that?"

"I didn't tell you?" he said and parked at the second corner. "We'll keep an eye open here."

"When?" I asked.

"He came to see me, I told you that. Watch across there."

"Yeah, that's right," I said. "There's something fishy about the whole thing. But why the hell do I care?"

"I told him nothing doing," Tom-tom said. "I told him for all I know you are not Tambor."

"Who's Tambor?" I said. "Who's got such a weird name?"

"*He* is," Tom-tom said. "He played the drums once, so they say, who knows."

"Yeah, I know what the word means," I said. (*Tambor* means drums.)

I cannot say why, but I thought of Longfellow. His readers sent him so many gifts that he had a thank-you card printed. And here I was, at the same venerable age, translating not Dante but Tom-tom.

"Well, he knocked on the door one day while I was out back and I found Olivia talking to him after I noticed a van parked on the street. That's why I know it was his van. OK? I got a good look at it and I am not forgetting it."

This time it was I who reached out and poked his shoulder. "There must be a shorter version of his visit. A *Reader's Digest* version."

"See across the street?" he said. "That's the Silver Dollar."

The Silver Dollar was catty-corner to us. Exactly what its corny name sounds like—a corner bar. Dirtier, I am sure, than the night's shadows allowed us to see. More ragged and dilapi-

dated than the moonlight's silver glaze promised. Three or four
men were leaning against a boarded-up window to one side of
the wide door at the corner. This entrance was open, a gaping
hole with no screen doors, and the lights inside were dim except
for a Budweiser neon sign that a salesman must have been mad
to place there. It surely could have had no effect on sales. All in
all, I would say drugs, not liquor, was the number one grosser
here.

A woman came to the door, paused with a hand on her hips,
and appeared to be looking at us. A man followed, rubbed
against her, and with mock scurrying, as if she might chase
him, went up the street. She or he laughed—or maybe one of
the men leaning against the building—a short, unenergetic,
genderless laugh.

The Silver Dollar and surroundings looked to me like the set
of a realistic movie about a southwestern town—or any small
town west of New York—the kind you say to yourself, my God,
it looks too real. They've shot it in an actual town in Texas and
they give thanks to it in the credits, but why do people live
there? Actually, it's not real: just a figment of the imagination of
a New York Jew.

"I see it," I said to Tom-tom, "but I don't believe it," trying
out my idea on him.

"You'd better believe it," he said. "There's all kinds of things
going on in there."

"Hey," the woman called.

We got nervous, both of us.

Why does a whore's approach always make you nervous?

Tom-tom looked at me and put on his sly smile. He said,
"See, you still good looking."

"Why are we stopping here?" I said.

"He mighta come here," Tom-tom said.

"Tom-tom, this is probably somebody else's turf," I said.

The woman started toward us.

"You know what I said means?" I said.

"I watch TV, my friend," he said, "and don't worry about that whore—I'll act like she's trying to rent apartments."

"I mean, he can't be around here doing business—of any kind," I said, to make sure. "Let's get away."

But the whore was upon us. She was being played by Cloris Leachman: skinny, harder than she should be, her voice so piercing that you knew it had been trained. Or she did a lot of practicing.

"Hiyas, fellas," she actually said. "How about a little fun? If you're the fuzz, that was just a friendly question. Passing the time."

"No fun for us tonight," I said.

"Is that so?" she said.

Tom-tom said, "We're waiting for some guy."

"You get your kicks that way?" she said. She laughed; it was a kind of cough.

"Which way?" Tom-tom asked.

"I was fooling," she said. "You too burly to be la-de-la."

"Too ugly, you mean, huh?" Tom-tom said.

I laughed.

"He's a card," she said to me. She saw no encouragement there. "OK," she said and tapped the car lightly. "What a night. See ya."

"See a van come by?" Tom-tom said.

She looked at him for a second to let him know she was getting into no trouble and then shook her head. "See you when you're horny," she said and gave a little fling to her ass as she turned away.

"I'll bet she was something when she was young," Tom-tom said.

"You know you don't believe that," I said.

"Pinpin, you gotta relax," he said. "You gotta go along more with what people say. You'll give yourself a heart attack, this way you have."

"We were all something when we were young," I said.

"That's true," he said, going along with me. He hung his arms on the steering wheel and looked desultorily up and down the street.

"That guy isn't going to come here," I said. "I mean that Tambor. Not if he knows his business."

"Looking for a customer, that's why he would come," Tom-tom said, "and then drive him somewhere. Oh, my poor Dulcie!"

"Those guys are looking for a high," I said. There was now a fifth skinny man leaning against the brick wall. "Look at them."

I stopped talking because it seemed to me that I was writing dialogue for a TV cop drama and not telling Tom-tom what was on my mind. I want to go to the old house in Ybor City, I want to go to sleep, I want to be more alone than Garbo. That's what was on my mind, and instead I was writing bad sides.

"Yeah, they don't look like they can get it up any more," Tom-tom said. "But who says that Tambor is smart? If he was smart he'd stay in Cuba."

"You and I are the only people in this benighted country who believe that," I said. "And I'm not so sure about you."

"You think I want to be worrying about renting my apartments? I don't want to write letters to the Traffic Department and dealing with filth like this we're waiting for," he said.

"It keeps you busy," I said.

"And Olivia, it wouldn't cost us a penny for all those allergy treatments if we lived in Cuba," he said. "Not a penny and no rent and Olivia could learn to read and write."

"What about McDonald's?" I said.

"I listen to Radio Havana," he said. "They're not starving there."

"Oh, shut up," I said. "I'm glad one person in the family believes in what grandpa did."

Nothing changed at the Silver Dollar.

*   *   *

I believed. Oh, I believed as fervently as a gospel singer. And I hated the enemies of socialism. Do I believe still? I have no beliefs, but I give up none of my hatreds. Especially my political hates. Still, there was more than hatred to look back on: December 1960 in Cuba was the grand moment of my life. In the tide of the Cubans' happiness Cora and I were young again. We are walking in Old Havana near Sloppy Joe's and we are so high that we don't know if we are hungry. Should we go over to La Bodeguita and eat or amble down to the harbor? I call out to a man on the corner—a black man in a panama hat and an immaculate *guayabera*—and when he turns to me with the gaiety and grace natural to a Havanan I ask for the time. He looks at the gold watch gleaming on his deep chocolate wrist. "One o'clock," he says, smiling so broadly that all his gold fillings wink at us, "revolutionary time!"

Sitting there in Tom-tom's funky car I could remember why I resisted visiting Tampa in the past. A few days ago, when I decided to come, I tried to remember why and could not. That's what I'm like since I hit sixty. Or was it sixty-two? I forget small things, unimportant details. Good, I said to myself, less dross. Then thought: but they're the stuff of life to a writer and to ordinary human beings. New York intellectuals are all abstract thinkers—if you can call them thinkers.

Where was I?

Why I did not come to Tampa: it made me forget who I was.

In this town I am only somebody's cousin. Tonight Tom-tom's. Tomorrow Marina's. But what the hell, everybody forgot who I was, anyway. I always lived in the past or future. I turned to Tom-tom; he was my present.

I said, "So what did you and that Tambor talk about? You had never met him, right? Why didn't you know about Dulcie after he left? What did he want from you? Don't slip away from me. You've got nothing to lose—or gain—by some plain truthful talking, Tom-tom. Keep me awake."

I leaned my head back on the seat, and waited.

"You think I know?" he said, sounding like a New York Jewish waiter.

I said, "Don't answer a question with a question. Just tell me the story—it will interest me. It'll pass the time."

"Pass the time," he repeated.

I said no more.

"And I thought you were a person who sympathizes," he said.

I said, "What happened to compassion?"

He didn't hear me. "You want me to come right out with it?"

The evening had cooled. It was like a late August night in Maine, this Florida late fall. I knew that in his view Tom-tom was fooling me, getting away with something, bolstering his self-image. Bolstering his self-image—what a trendy way to express a simple feeling. On a page I'd never let it get past a first draft. But I am an ex-writer now, I can relax, like an aunt of mine who in old age would push her false teeth forward and back with her tongue, sometimes grinning when they were mostly out, and giving the kids a good laughing scare.

I felt at ease. Blameless. Living in the present. I was doing a good deed for Tom-tom. Had I levitated at the McDonald's parking lot? I was above it all now, impervious to my hometown and to humanity as well. I was cool, man.

"He said Dulcie was back in Texas, that's what he said to Olivia and to me too," Tom-tom said, sounding as devious and worried as ever. "In fact, I think he said Dulcie was staying with her mother while he was away."

"Did he really?" I said. "Maybe she is."

"No!" he said impatiently.

He looked over at the Silver Dollar and then back at me. He opened his mouth a couple of times, not in the eager way that he closed in on the french fries but hesitantly, indecisively.

"You the only one in the family with no prejudices," he said. "Celia, your own sister, said that you went over once to see Trafficante. You weren't prejudiced that he's big-time Mafia."

Despite myself I began to get apprehensive again.

"Or was that what I told my brother Ralph, you remember him and his baseball ambitions? He came over with his stories about Dulcie," he said, then chuckled or burped or sighed. No, it was too strangled a sound for a sigh. "I told him only Pinpin in our whole family got no prejudices."

After another moment of my lying back with my head on the seat and not prodding him, he said, "You can't tell all the truth, you know."

"No, you cannot," I replied, also after a moment.

I closed my eyes to check if I was ready for sleep. I saw Cora's face and she was telling me she was going to New York Hospital. Just overnight, she said; so casually I knew she was covering up. She knew I had a lunch date with a *Times Magazine* editor that day, the first lunch with an editor I had been able to wangle with no effort in two years. I had said to her, Do you think left-wingers are back? She saw me think all this and said, before I could turn my good intentions into speech, I don't need you to come along. And I said . . .

I opened my eyes: I preferred to be with Tom-tom. I must live in the little present left to me. I rolled my head slightly to the left in order to look at the Silver Dollar.

Tom-tom shifted his body to face me and his face was like a close-up in an old Garbo movie—huge. This was the position for close petting when I was in high school. I was somewhat alarmed but immediately recovered: the advent of sex always unnerved me, but that I should respond like that with Tom-tom was funny.

"Pinpin, Pinpin," he whispered.

"What's the matter?" I said.

"I think I knew he had brought Dulcie with him."

"So?"

"I mean that he had brought her from Texas," he said. "I don't want you to think I lie to you."

"OK," I said.

"He didn't bring her along with him that night, because he had something serious to discuss with me. He said that and the way he looked at Olivia she got up and went to the kitchen to make coffee."

He opened his eyes wide but he wasn't watching me. "I don't know why she did that. I wish she didn't do that! I can't get over it. I told her we wouldn't be in all this trouble if she hadn't left me alone with him."

Now he studied me again.

"Why?" I said. "Where'd she go?"

"I told you," he said. "To the kitchen, to make coffee."

"But couldn't she hear from there?"

"He whispered all the time, the son of a bitch."

"Well, that doesn't sound dangerous to me. If he attacked you, you could've called her," I said, why I don't know, but I was still feeling the good of the levitation at McDonald's.

"Because he has a smooth tongue, like all those Cuban refugees," Tom-tom said. "She coulda stopped me if she heard."

"Out with it," I said, and I tried smiling his sly smile right into his big, flabby, overused face.

"Ay, Pinpin, you're too smart to fool," he said. "He talked me into giving him a thousand dollars!"

I puckered my lips to whistle the way we whistled when we were kids every time someone told us a whopper. I couldn't. So I said, "How'd he do that?"

"You saw how my sister got the apartment outa me and I didn't even tell that gigolo Felo off. I got a good heart. It's a curse."

"That's my trouble too," I said, but it was lost on him.

He said, "There, I told you," and smiled his sly smile. "You are the only person I told."

I winked his wink. "So you're not out to save Dulcie—you want your thousand dollars back, that's all."

I kept my eyes on him and I swear he turned pale, though I can't say how I could have known in that dim light inside the car. But there was no mistaking the tautness that pulled his sagging face smooth: shock and fear. Fear that I'd leave him?

I was going to apologize, but he beat me to the punch: he began to cry.

Shit, why do people aspire to authenticity?

I shall say for myself (since I am not looking for approval) that I picked up the phone and dialed the *Times* to call off the appointment to be able to go, instead, to the hospital with Cora. It was the first of many trips and I always accompanied her, except on those occasions when in her Waspish way she went off alone without telling me. But I was a Latin from Ybor City and there was buried deep within me the belief that you went to the hospital to die and that the neighbors would comment adversely if you let the patient go alone or, while there, remain alone without an incompetent family member to stand watch. I would dash up to Sixty-eighth Street as soon as I checked her calendar and saw that's where she had gone.

I did not expect Cora to smile or thank me when I caught up with her. She had cancer, why should she be grateful? Still, I felt a pang of neglect and had to correct myself without a word when she did not thank me more than once, as a Latin would have done.

When it came to the radiation sessions, she needed someone along, and I did not let Susie take my place.

Needless to say, I did not go near Susie during those days. Even when Ira was a world away and the opportunities were many. Which is why it was inevitable I should later.

"Isn't Ira away?" Cora asked once.

What did she mean? I asked myself. But I said, "Didn't he call you from Florida?"

"Every day," she said and went back to her murder mystery.

I blushed.

I said, "Cora, that was a long time ago."

She kept her head down. I saw a tear drop into her paperback. Then another.

Jesus Christ, I would kill Susie if she told her we had resumed. Kick her ass in.

I said, "Believe me."

"I believe you," she said.

And a stone rolled off my chest.

"It does not matter, anyway," she said.

"No?" I said, wary.

"I cannot expect an artist to be a good bourgeois," she said.

"Oh, Cora, you're the only woman in New York—anywhere—who'd say that," I said. It was the first time in a week I forgot she had cancer. "What would the feminists say?"

"I am not a feminist," she said with her old strength. "Socialism is the issue."

"Yes," I said. "Goddamnit." My throat constricted; I almost cried.

When I could speak, I said, "You're going to be all right, you know."

She said, "Well, we saw Cuba, didn't we?"

That killed me, all right, all right, all right.

As in a romantic painting, the sun came out just as it was going down, and a ray of it, yellowish as always at the end of day, lit her where she sat by the window. It turned her into the smooth-haired Veronica Lake blond I first knew. I loved her and had lost the way of saying it.

"Oh, Cora," I said.

"The whole island was beautiful, wasn't it!" she said. She threw up her arms in celebration of our days together in Cuba and brought them down quickly because of the pain.

"Yes," I said.

"Make it up with them," she said.

How did she know I longed to? My mouth dropped open, I swear. I had been wanting to go back to Havana without in any way admitting that I was softening my stand about their having jailed a poet who was a friend of mine. (Actually, he was not much of a friend.) And Cora had given me the perfect excuse: my sick wife had asked me to return—I could not well refuse her.

"You're right, Cora," I said. "I'll go back and write a piece that will turn around all the anti-Cuban stuff the intellectuals are . . . you know."

She looked up and smiled her wide smile and I placed my hand on her hair and smoothed it the way I did once. The sun withdrew its gold at that moment and it was gray hair my mottled, thickened hand fingered.

She pretended to be better so that I should feel free to call the Cubans for a visa. Her doctor was an old friend of hers and she counted on his cooperation, but he called me to say that he knew I would want to know that she had asked him to tell me that she was in remission. I stopped myself from calling Susie to discuss it with her: it was my declaration of faith in Cora that I consulted only my own feelings in staying. Childishly, I thought: No one will know of my good deed.

Cora faced me cheerfully each day and walked about the apartment with the springiness of a girl of her class playing tennis. "I cannot wait for you to come back and tell me about the new work schools," she said. "I'll have so many questions to ask you."

I called the Cuban Mission to the United Nations to keep her happy. I asked for the ambassador, and in the past the ambassador would come right on and say, "Pack up—I'll telegraph and your visa will be at the Mexico City consulate in two days.

I'll also tell them to reserve a room at the Nacional, right?"

He was not in. His secretary was new and asked for my number. I told her he had it, but gave it to her anyway. She did not call back.

I did not mean to go, so it was a couple of days before I noticed. The boys had flown in from L.A. to confer with a director in New York who went west only in time for the first day of shooting. (I did not believe them and Cora very likely did not either.) There was much jollity. They insisted on staying at our apartment instead of the Carlyle and they occupied their old rooms, now lined with all those Riverside editions I made Cora fight for when her father died. This was the first time the boys had been downtown in years. I exaggerate.

"God, the Village is great now," Jared said, as soon as they had taken their first walk.

They took us to the nearby grand places—La Tulipe, Texarkana, the Gotham—since they believed Cora's pretense that she was feeling just fine. Or did they?

I called the ambassador again. His secretary asked me to repeat my name. "And you are calling in relation to what?" she said in a tone I did not like.

"A visa," I said.

"The ambassador does not issue visas," she said. "You may wish to apply to the Cuban Interests Office in Washington."

Abjectly, I pleaded, "The ambassador knows me."

"I shall give him your message," she said, and hung up.

Cora and the boys were in the living room talking about the boat races in Maine and recalling dear old Cap'n Cole, a begrimed, dissembling souse who fooled all the summer people into believing he was the salt of the earth. Irritating that Cora and the boys should have been taken in too and made him part of their, as we used to say, *Weltanschauung*. Typically Wasp. That's what I thought as I came away from the phone in my study.

"When are you leaving, pop?" asked Crispin.

Jared said, "I forgot to tell you, dad. When we pitched our last story to the head of production, he said before we started, I liked your old man's book on Cuba. He said that!"

"I don't give a shit what the head of production thinks," I said. "If he thinks."

"Ha-ha!" Crispin laughed; he was always the placator.

Not Jared. "He was SDS strike committee in the Sixties—he's OK. He paid his dues."

"He's a vulgarian, isn't he?" I said. "What dues? What's that?"

Cora asked, "Didn't you reach him?"

"Who?" I said.

"The Cuban ambassador," she said, as if she didn't know I was about to explode. "I thought you went in to call him."

"Stop stalking me," I said.

"Yeah, dad, we're all rooting for you," Crispin said.

"You're rooting for me!" I said.

"Me, I don't care," Jared said; he was the younger one, the tougher one, the one who liked Cora.

"What's the matter?" Cora asked—persistence and directness come with money and assurance.

"Mom, dad's a writer," Crispin said. "We hate to be cornered. We're an unpredictable bunch."

"Writers!" I yelled. "What the fuck do you two know about writing? You punch computers. I never saw a paragraph written by either of you, not a sentence. Never a letter home. You don't need to write a complete sentence to punch out one of your scripts—Enter asshole, spouting shit! Blah, blah, blah!"

Crispin got up; he had paled. He was the older one and I had kicked him in the ass when he tried adolescent rebellion on us. He was scared of me, even now. His mouth opened and closed and nothing came out.

Jared spoke for him. "This is uncalled for."

"Get outa here," I said. "Exit."

Cora insisted. "Did you talk to the ambassador? Why are you upset?"

I let go. "Why don't you talk to him? You're one of those American social-minded ladies on their mailing list. I know the goddamn mail you get. And I've seen you snub Mary McCarthy every summer of our lives because she's a Trotskyite, you say, but really because she's not Back Bay, Beacon Hill, Louisburg Square like dear dead Cal Lowell! And the Party? Surely they can—they can come to the aid of your party."

"Dad," said Crispin, "you're not supposed to get upset like this."

"You ask them for a visa. You're no persona non grata," I yelled at Cora. "See where all your loyalty gets you—you give them a suitable donation every year. Not too much, mind you—we mustn't be vulgar about money. You've never had a critical response in forty years—"

"Cut it out," Jared said. "You're supposed to be the big Third World revolutionary writer."

"Shut up, you dumb Wasp," I said. "Go punch your computer."

"Dad!" Crispin said. "Don't get upset."

"I'm not upset," I said and tried to get past Cora to my study. "I simply tell the truth."

"Did you take your medicine?" Cora asked, reaching out with one hand to keep me there.

She was maddening, maddening.

"That's all I've ever done—taken my medicine. Take your medicine, don't upset the children, don't give the class enemy comfort!"

All the clichés are true: you see stars when you bump your head, you see red when you've been insulted and rejected—the real emotional you.

I turned on the boys: "So, are you sound, in touch with yourselves, psychologically unharmed, keeping your portfolios well balanced?"

"Fuck it," Jared said, still fighting me. I saw his eyes glisten and thought of smacking him one.

"Whoa, Jed," Crispin said.

Cora picked up the *Times*.

"Change your names," I said. "Or you'll be taken for upwardly mobile Puerto Ricans."

"I might just do that," Jared said. He looked over at Cora. "Mom? Hey, mom, maybe we could—"

"Go to a hotel," I said.

Cora held up a hand and for the first time in front of the children a tear ran down her cheek.

"I'm going for a walk," I said, looking at a nowhere spot between my idiot sons. "And when I come back I want you both out of here. Call before you ever visit again. I don't want to see you."

I had a hand on the door. It was all wildly unsatisfactory, unrounded. I had to say or do something definitive. I looked back at them and said, "And when *I'm* dying I want no pretenses." And I slammed the door behind me.

But I could hear Jared's voice calling, "You son of a bitch, you're no father of mine!"

Tom-tom cried not because he had been fooled into giving Tambor money that was to, in a roundabout way, help Dulcie back in Texas but because he had made a deal with Tambor and Tambor had reneged. The deal was that Tambor would use the thousand to buy cocaine and the return for Tom-tom, after Tambor sold it to his customers, would be ten thousand.

It did not take me long to get that out of him, maybe because of the hour or because of my live-and-let-live attitude (and it is true that I didn't care) or because all along he had wanted to confess to me and be pardoned. In any case, he stopped beating around the bush and answered my questions straight.

Who knows, I might yet confess to him that my sons hated me.

"And besides this ten thousand to you," I asked, "he was also making a profit?"

Tom-tom glued his tear-wet face into mine. "You think that's too much?"

"You don't?" I said. "Who were his customers? I guess you wouldn't know that."

"Why you trying to make me into some smalltown hick?" he said, aggrieved again. "I'm your cousin."

"My greedy cousin," I said.

"How many times I hafta tell you?" he said. "I did it to help Dulcie, to help their marriage."

"And the ten thousand?" I said. "You didn't do it for that?"

I did not mean to use a penny of Cora's money that after my death was to go to the boys. I told the Boston executor to plow back (that was *his* verb) the income into the mutual funds or whatever it was all a parcel of. They could've saved all those maneuvers to avoid double inheritance taxes. Let it all go immediately to them. Wasp money to Wasps. I'd do nothing for money. Publication, awards, honorific titles, I'd kiss ass for that but never much got the chance.

I insisted Tom-tom answer. "The ten thousand from cocaine," I said. "For you, right?"

"I was going to give it to them," he said in a kind of spasm, as if even the thought of parting with that amount cost him a physical effort.

"You don't have to explain," I said. "I don't give a shit. Just assure me there's no cocaine in this car."

"In this car!"

"I don't want any troubles with the authorities," I explained. "Peace in my last days—that's all I want."

That now familiar squeeze of the heart. My pig valve giving out? Or did I now need a bypass?

"I have never been mixed up in stuff like that," Tom-tom said. "Sell drugs, never."

"And what do you think you were doing with Tambor?"

"I was just giving him money," he said and grabbed my arm and held on. "That's all I was doing, helping him out."

"Let go," I said, but I could only manage it in a whisper and he still squeezed and brought his face closer.

"He was the only one who was handling the drugs," he said. "For all I know, it coulda been something else. Maybe it was just my imagination it was cocaine. I didn't really know, come to think of it."

I could not speak, I only stared at him and hoped that he would loosen the tourniquet on my arm.

He relented a little. "Well, I figured it was drugs because of the high rate of profit."

"High rate of profit," I repeated, but did not have the extra breath to laugh.

"Why you making fun of me?" he said. "I'm your own flesh and blood."

He let go of my arm and I could feel a tingling in my hand with the restored circulation.

I saw the man go up to the others at the Silver Dollar. He was Cuban; I knew that immediately and I cannot explain why: the way he held himself and moved, as if all his brain cells were in his balls.

I did not know Cora was on chemotherapy until her hair fell out. She had all sorts of Russian kerchiefs she now wore; English paisleys, too; Mexican bandannas; Chilean scarfs so tightly woven by Mapuche women they were rain-proof; all of them accumulated during her membership in a thousand political delegations to one new country or the other. The executive boards of the committees that sent her to them began coming to our apartment, holding some of their meetings there. Women's support groups never left her alone a moment. Cora bought a cordless phone which she kept at her side and I was lucky enough not to have picked it up when my so-called sons called from the Coast. Once a day I remembered Jared's loud execration: you son of a bitch, you're no father of mine. But on the whole Cora smoothed out those last weeks for me; I didn't even quite know they were the last weeks.

But she finally died and her body went off to the crematorium. There was no service of any kind. That's how she wanted it. Thank God. I went home. I put on the telephone answering machine and paid no attention to its rings, but the next evening there was knocking at the door. I could hear Crispin but he finally went away. In the morning, I took a suitcase and went to the Gramercy Park Hotel, and a week later I came home still in a daze. The answering machine contained several calls from Crispin and a couple from Susie. One from Jared asking my forgiveness. One from the lawyers in Boston. I gave up: I called Susie and I went uptown to see her, half wanting a roll in bed, and was met by Ira. He hugged me: to make a short story shorter, their idea of comfort was to make a threesome in their bed. I went up to Boston to the lawyer; he was bracingly cool. I hated them all. Especially the Boston lawyer in whom I heard the voice of America apportioning ancestral and economic justice.

I pointed to the Silver Dollar. "Who's that guy?" I said.

"It's him!" Tom-tom said and his shirt got caught on the steering wheel and tore as he propelled himself out. "What shall I do?"

He fell to his knees on the street. Not to pray but inadvertently. He got up and I could hear him panting. "Help me, Pinpin."

I opened the door on my side, caught my foot between the car and the curb, and fell on sand and that harsh grass they call lawn in Florida and picked up the inevitable pricking sand spurs of my youth. "Cora," I said as if she were there to help, and got up the faster for that slip.

I had watched Tom-tom skip and waddle and thrash his arms as if they were propellers but he had yet to make it to the Silver Dollar when I got up. A car honked. The Cuban turned around.

"Hey, you!" Tom-tom called.

The Cuban froze.

"Tambor," Tom-tom said. He was at the curb of the Silver Dollar but had to pause. "I want a word with you."

Tambor peered. "Who you?" he asked, but he began to move away.

"Stop him," Tom-tom said to the men at the wall. "Catch him."

Fat chance. They didn't move. Couldn't.

Tambor cursed and I started across the street. He saw Tom-tom but not me. He ran away from the street lights into the shadows of the old oaks up the street. The old houses there were boarded up and no light from them penetrated the gloom.

"Don't go there," I called after Tom-tom.

I looked at the men at the Silver Dollar. They looked back and they were neither hot nor cold.

"Be careful, Tom-tom," I called again. "Come back."

"Hey, mister," one man called in the most disinterested voice I ever heard. "The fella's just a pimp, he don't want any trouble. He's one of them Cubans. Don't know his way round."

Then it was true about Dulcie.

I said, "Thank you."

Tom-tom came back. "I don't see where he coulda gone," he said and looked hopefully at the alcoholic who had spoken to me. "No noise of a car?"

"Is he working out of a house here?" I said, addressing the same skinny man too. He looked like Walter Brennan but he spoke much less. "He's got a van?"

That was the end of the questioning. Walter Brennan took out a knife and began to work on his nails. I almost laughed. The others all shuffled a little, a mere shift of a leg at most, while Tom-tom and I played out our scene. "Let's go back," I said and they all relaxed and leaned against the wall again.

We heard, highly magnified, the morning cough of a two-pack-a-day smoker. Aroused, Tom-tom grabbed me. "It's a car," he said and looked up the street. "He's taking off!"

He hurried back to his car. "Come on," he said and waved for me without looking back. "We'll lose them."

"At 'em, cowboy," someone behind us said, but we did not bother to answer.

I jogged after Tom-tom feeling like an old fool, but not he: his heart was in it, waddle and all, he didn't care if he was a spectacle.

He flooded the carburetor. (I love that phrase.) He counted to ten and it caught the second time. He turned down the street that Tambor had run.

"There's nothing, there's nothing," he said, peering.

"Put on your lights," I said, my face at the windshield, "and don't stop suddenly."

"Oh God, I forgot," he said, and the lights came on.

Big oaks, the big oaks of our childhood, one car parked at the next corner. Boarded houses. Tall weeds. For Rent signs. A high mound started at the end of the street a block away.

"What's that?" I said.

"What? What?"

"There, there, ahead."

"You mean the freeway?" He licked his lips in order to speak, he was so scared. "All these streets are dead end until MacDill."

He flung an arm descriptively and hit my nose. "The freeway cuts across."

He turned south and we looked at the next dead-end block. He slowed down at each corner; our headlights didn't illuminate sideways and we could not always see the full length of the block to the freeway's hillock. "Can you see?" he asked at the second block with desperation.

I looked out my side window, my heart thumping. "No, no," I said, saw some chic signs, and added, "The two houses are offices." Darkness beyond. "Wait."

He waited.

"No, there's no car."

He took off for the next street. The same questions, the same answers. The car lights went off.

"Why ya turning off the lights?" I said. "Tom-tom, the lights."

A loud whisper from him: "I don't wanna let him know I'm coming."

"What about other cars?"

"That's their lookout," he said impatiently. He rolled to the next corner. "Besides, you see better in the dark."

He was right.

Looking down on us at the corner, one of the grand old houses, restored. A free-standing sign on the sidewalk, in tasteful lettering, announced a firm of lawyers.

"What's that?" I said and pointed to the corner across from the lawyers' offices.

A two-story bulk, that's all I could make out. Its edges moved and blurred, I swear. A spook house in a cartoon.

"The old firehouse," Tom-tom said, and prodded me to make me look down the dead-end block.

"But it moves," I said.

"I'm blind, I'm blind," he said, peering beyond me. "I can't see a thing."

I was mesmerized by the moving monster that he called the firehouse. Was it hung with outside draperies?

"It moves, I tell you," I said.

"A termite tent," Tom-tom said, his turn to be irritable. "Look the other way. What do you see?"

"On a three-story building?" I said. "A termite tent?"

"Jesus," he said. "They sold the firehouse and the termites are all over it. They put a tent on it, pump in poison gas and let it stay a couple of nights. Now, Pinpin, is there anyone down the block?"

The high slope to the freeway again. One, two, three cars went by on the freeway but the street remained dark. Then a truck with big headlights came by above the hillock and its lights made enough of an illumined backdrop to let me see, in the foreground of the street, one parked car and beyond it, where the wire fence to the freeway's slope began, the humped outline of a van.

"It's there," I said.

"It's there?" Tom-tom said.

"I think so."

"But is it a van?"

I nodded.

"What?"

I nodded again.

"What?"

I realized it was too dark for him to see me nod and this time I whispered, "Yes!"

"Yes, a van?"

I started to nod again. "Yes, for chrissakes," I said. "A van."

He grabbed his head with both hands.

I said, "What do we do now?" and quickly felt ashamed: it would have been so much easier on both of us if we hadn't found Tambor.

"I'm gonna go look," Tom-tom said.

This time it was me who grabbed his arm. He didn't move, he didn't flinch, he didn't want to go.

I whispered, "Roll the car to the middle of the street."

He looked at me as if I were mad.

"That way he can't make a U-turn and get out of the block. Not with the van."

Thank God he had not turned off the ignition. First, he put it in neutral, but there was no slant to the street and the old wreck stayed put. Then, on first.

I said, "Slow with the gas."

"Shush," he whispered.

"I'm the one who's telling you to be quiet!" I whispered back, but intensely. The damn fool. I looked towards the slope of the freeway; the van sat at its bottom playing possum. "Wait," I said. "Put it in neutral again."

I got out of the car slowly, left the door open to make no noise, and went to the back, placed a hand on either side of the back trunk lock, and pushed. The car did not move. I leaned against it and rested. That invisible hand squeezed my heart again.

Tom-tom put it in first (I could feel the thump of the car changing gears as I could my arthritic knee on a cloudy day) and fed it gas. The exhaust pipe sent up a puff of pollution straight to my nostrils and I stumbled after the car. He stopped it smack in the middle of the old, narrow street. Tambor would never get out; he'd have to fly.

I made a gesture to Tom-tom—both hands palms out and a pushing motion—to urge him to stay behind the wheel. I walked over and leaned with an arm above his door and took a deep breath to get the fumes out of my lungs.

"He didn't see me back at the Silver Dollar," I said. "Whyn't I go over and talk to him and see what's doing?"

He reached behind him for the rifle.

"You gotta promise me," I said. "Leave that there. No violence."

He placed the rifle between his legs and turned to me. "I promise, Pinpin, I don't use it," he said. "Unless."

"No unless," I said.

"It's not loaded," he said and gave me his sly smile.

"For chrissakes," I said. "I'm going over."

He reached out the window and grabbed me. "What you gonna do?"

"I am going to pretend I'm out for a walk," I said, "and see what he says."

"Out for a walk here?" he said.

"Yeah, here."

He sighed.

I left him and headed for the sidewalk with the lawyers' sign. The block was only about one-third the length it had been before the freeway. No signs of life in the van, but my palms were sweaty and I knew it was fear that made them so. I rubbed my hands on my Brooks chinos. Nothing to be afraid of from these worms; they all ran at the Bay of Pigs.

It had a Texas license, all right. I walked by it, no more than a couple of feet away, and heard nothing; but then my hearing wasn't what it used to be.

As I passed the front window, I did an eyes-left and saw Tambor (I guessed) at the wheel smoking a cigarette. He was startled, I could tell, for his cigarette stopped in mid-air, and I found the nerve to nod to him. He did not respond (probably too surprised to do so) and I had to keep going toward the slope. I felt like a dope when I got to it a few paces later; I simply stood there and looked up its incline at the low railing up there. One car went by, that's all; after nine o'clock Tampa is still a small town.

So what do I do now?

I turned around to walk back. Tambor was out of the van

standing in front of it still smoking, his lips moving, trying to form some words, ready to talk as soon as I came closer. He was at a loss, like me, for an opening gambit.

He smiled.

I nodded.

"Hey, mister," he said and got up on the sidewalk. "Is a good night, right?"

I nodded and said, "Yep."

He looked around, gave a little laugh. "You ready for some action?"

"Me?" I said.

"Hell, you young, man," he said, but it came out listless and tentative.

He was scared, the lousy bastard. He wore jeans, but he moved and stood like a Parque Central bum in Old Havana.

"Young for what?" I said.

But my English was too rapid for him.

"Me, young?" He looked up and down, perplexed, and then got a self-assured smile and gave me a wink. "No me, man, a girl I got."

"A girl? Where?" I said, even more self-assured than he—I wasn't going to be taken for an old aunty.

"You like that, huh, is a honey pot," he said, sounding like an obscene "I Love Lucy" show. He leered. "Nookey, nookey, fresh meat."

"Where?" I repeated.

He indicated the van with a move of his head.

"You hot, hot."

His fake, unwavering grin showed both a gold tooth and a gap.

"You no cocksucker, you a cunt licker, OK." He winked. He threw away his cigarette and feinted with the same hand as if he were going to grab my crotch.

Naturally, I jumped back.

"You no cocksucker," he repeated. He got closer and while looking at the van to show he was describing his goods, whispered, "I need money is why. She my personal girl. Sixteen."

"Sixteen!" I said. "What do you take me for?"

"No, no, I say eighteen. Is legal."

So what do I do now?

My wavering showed. He grabbed my shirt. "Maybe you cocksucker." He reached around roughly for my ass. "Costs more." He laughed and grabbed. It hurt.

I pushed with both hands. I put all my strength into it; I was amazed that he fell back. I felt a strange thrill go through me and lodge in my heart.

"No like?" he said and placed a hand on his hip, and there, in its leather holder, was a knife like those the country boys in Maine carried to look macho. He unsnapped the small strap that went round the wide handle. "You not mug me, right?"

He pulled out the knife.

"Is self-defense, no?"

He smiled. He put the knife back, but did not strap it in. He said, "Listen, mister, don't worry. No harm, never. I no mug, police don't care, huh? You fuck my girl, they no care. OK?"

I said, "Is your girl in there?"

He looked up and down the block and saw Tom-tom's car. It looked empty from where we stood. He looked at me.

"My car," I said, wondering where Tom-tom hid his bulk. He frowned.

"Ran out of gas," I said. "Help me push it?"

I don't know how I thought of that.

"After," he said.

"You gonna show me the girl?" I said.

"You like, eh?" He showed me the gap and the gold tooth

and feigned another grab at my crotch. "Ha-ha, in car."

I followed him to the back of the van. He didn't scare me, and I moved, as my heart felt, detached from everything around me. I touched the van to test it was there.

"Money first," he said, one hand on the back door.

"Why?" I said.

He shrugged.

"How do I know you got a girl there or if I like her?"

"You no trust me?" he said and quickly added, "OK, OK, we make price first."

"Whaddya want?" I said; I felt like bashing his face and destroying his Desi Arnaz accent.

"Fifty dollars," he said.

"What!" I said.

"I push your car too," he said.

"Forty," he bargained.

"Let's have a look," I said. "I'm promising nothing."

He unlocked the door with his left hand and pulled it back slightly. In his right hand he flashed the knife again. "The money," he said.

I stared at the knife. He stared at me.

"I haven't seen what I'm getting," I said, scared and losing breath. Through the slit of the open door I could see a naked foot. It was dirty, the bottom black. I said slowly to make sure he understood. "I wanna see."

"OK," he said, then shook his head. "No feel."

There she was, and the half-light must have helped her looks. A cotton frock—is that the right word for a house dress that should long ago have been used to wet-mop the patio?—and no more. Her legs were up and bent and the dress had rolled back and even in the dim light I could see she wore nothing underneath. Her tits made two points in the dress. Her eyes were close together, and she directed a quizzical, puzzled expression at me out of a half-sleep.

"Tambor," she said in a pleading whine. "I'm hungry."

Tambor crowded me, expecting his money, and I stepped back in horror—yes, in horror—to be able to slug him. He grabbed me with one hand, and thinking I had lost interest, with the other reached inside the van and pulled one of her legs aside.

"That's good pussy, man," he said. "Look."

I did look—no reason to explain why—and he was right, a pink, petulant mound and beckoning folded lips.

"Dulcie?" I said.

"I'm hungry," she said, acknowledging, I can't say how, that I had used her name. "I'm hungry."

I'll kill him—and did not have time to complete the thought. His face gleamed close to mine and his eyes widened with fear and evil. I must kill him, I must. He fisted my shirt again and as he slammed the van's door shut he pulled me back and forth, thumping my chest with the knuckles of his fist each time I lurched forward. Out of some primeval movie memory I bent a leg and lifted it with all my might and aimed for his crotch. The second door slammed at the same time, but I think he yelled in pain and he did let go of me—ho, ho!

He lifted a hand; it appeared aimed at my face. "I no say her name. Her name Maria!" And his hand started down on its parabola towards me.

I yelled, "Tom-tom!" and I threw myself at him and missed. I hit the ground but did not feel it. He ran to the front of the van and I dragged myself on the brick walk to see where he went. He opened the door and I yelled, "Tom-tom," as he looked back at our car. He slammed the door close and decided to run instead.

I got up in three moves, cursing my age, and once more yelled, "Tom-tom!" and only then realized that this time my voice worked. My throat burned with the effort I had made.

Tambor was running up the slope to the freeway. It slowed him and he looked back and waved and yelled, "No, no!" I looked back too and there was Tom-tom in the middle of the street aiming his rifle.

Tambor veered left and still yelling, "No, no!" ran into the yard of a boarded-up house across the street from me. I took after him. I was going to get him, I was going to kill him, if only my legs would move as they once did.

Bang! Just like that.

The report of Tom-tom's rifle did not shock me; it propelled me. All the evil in this world was in him: I'd get him, I'd get him.

"Pinpin, Pinpin, Pinpin!" The street echoed with my name. The heavenly choir celebrating me, me, me.

With one arm I thrashed the line of hibiscus bushes in the front yard of the house. I remembered his knife. I paused. I ran to the oleanders at the edge of the back porch. There was a tall fence—he could not escape into the next block through there. I saw his shadow run under the camphor tree heading for the menacing bulk of the old firehouse.

"Pinpin, come back!"

I knew it was Tom-tom, but I heard him only as sound. I did not catch its meaning; like song it fueled and lifted me across the backyard.

"Come back, come back . . ."

There was a space of moonlight between the lacy edge of the furthest branch of the camphor tree and the elephantine epidermis of the firehouse, and he paused, transfigured by its brilliance, his body emerging from the tall weeds, and he twisted his hips and his shoulders and turned and raised a hand holding the knife like a figure in hell, his legs enmeshed in the weeds that my hate turned into flames. He was the sinner in torment; I the archangel. He dived; I levitated. Into the thick, high curtains he went—no, no, they were canvas, I corrected myself, trying to descend into reality for I must no longer observe and curse but act. There goes Tambor, I must catch him.

Two Texas cowboy boots wriggling into the tent. I laughed and caught them and it was a joy. No bitterness but utter delight. Gary Cooper's boots! Gary Cooper's boots! The prize of my childhood! Cora joined me in laughter. I hung on and laughed. Hang on, she called, fight the good fight!

Yes, yes, yes. Know that I love you, Cora. Know that I always loved you. I yearned towards her and knew that the hands caressing my chest were Susie's not Cora's and both drew me into life. Yet above them I saw Cora and all was one and happiness and plenitude: my sons absolved and chanting, dad, dad, dad! Up there, Cora's face descending now, her eyes searching me out, her lips slightly open with love coming down to mine and the breath of her life in me. We were young and I ached for her. No holding back, no quarrels, all was one.

Thump. "Oh, I'm sorry," and a chanting uplifting count.

"No, darling, no apologies," I said, but I was not sure, as in a dream, that I said it and I tried again. "No apologies, darling, none, I love you."

Then like the soloist returning to the major key after his cadenza I heard the voice turn into Tom-tom's breathy gravel. "Two breaths again," he said and kissed me, I thought, on the lips.

Beyond him, Dulcie, more cockeyed in the moonlight than in the darkness of the van.

He lifted away and with his big warm hands pushed gently down on my chest and the chant of my sons turned into his anxious count again. I wanted to reassure him. There was Dulcie beside him, saved; he need not worry.

"Pinpin, Pinpin," he said as he pressed his bulk against me and open-mouthed came down to my lips again.

I loved him. I told him so.

His breath went through me twice and he lifted away.

"I love you, Pinpin," he said. His wonderful hands now simply rubbed my chest. "Rest. You're OK, the CPR worked. I learned it on TV."

He gave me his sly smile. "I got the keys to the van too!"

"I love you, Tom-tom," I said with all my senses this time. Dulcie said, "Who is he, Papa Tom-tom?"

"My cousin," Tom-tom said and stroked my head the way my mother once did. "Aunt Mama's son."

"What are you two doing in Texas?" she said.

Tom-tom took my hands and rubbed them. "We're in Tampa, honey."

"Goody," said Dulcie. "Home again."

I looked at their two loving faces and thought: America! But said nothing.